MATCHING
CAST ONS & BIND OFFS

MATCHING CAST ONS & BIND OFFS

Six Pairs of Methods
that Form Identical Cast On and Bind Off Edges
on Projects Knitted Flat and in the Round

Maryna Shevchenko

10 Rows a Day

Copyright © 2023 by Maryna Shevchenko

All rights reserved. Thank you for supporting the author's rights by buying an authorized copy of this book, and by not reproducing or distributing any part of it in any form without permission. To get the permission, please contact the author at maryna@10rowsaday.com.

www.10rowsaday.com

ISBN 978-1-7386402-2-5 paperback
ISBN 978-1-7386402-3-2 e-book

Cover design by:
Sasha Shevchenko
www.sasha-shevchenko.com

Published in Canada

To everyone
who finds joy in knitting

CONTENTS

INTRODUCTION 9
BASIC EDGES 10

Chain Cast On + Suspended Bind Off 10
    Chain Cast On Worked Flat 11
    Chain Cast On Worked in the Round 15
    Suspended Bind Off Worked Flat 16
    Suspended Bind Off Worked in the Round 24

Rolled Cast On + Rolled Bind Off 28
    Rolled Cast On Worked Flat 29
    Rolled Cast On Worked in the Round 32
    Rolled Bind Off Worked Flat 34
    Rolled Bind Off Worked in the Round 36

Tuck Cast On + Tuck Bind Off 38
    Tuck Cast On Worked Flat 39
    Tuck Cast On Worked in the Round 44
    Tuck Bind Off Worked Flat 47
    Tuck Bind Off Worked in the Round 52

Quick Reference Cards 55

I-CORD EDGES 61

I-Cord Cast On + I-Cord Bind Off 61
    I-Cord Cast On Worked Flat 62
    I-Cord Cast On Worked in the Round 68
    I-Cord Bind Off Worked Flat 79
    I-Cord Bind Off Worked in the Round 87

Purled I-Cord Cast On + Purled I-Cord Bind Off 94
    Purled I-Cord Cast On Worked Flat 95
    Purled I-Cord Cast On Worked in the Round 104
    Purled I-Cord Bind Off Worked Flat 117
    Purled I-Cord Bind Off Worked in the Round 122

Braided Cast On + Braided Bind Off 131
    Braided Cast On Worked Flat 132
    Braided Cast On Worked in the Round 138
    Braided Bind Off Worked Flat 147
    Braided Bind Off Worked in the Round 151

Quick Reference Cards 159

INTRODUCTION

When we inspect a designer sweater or cardigan, often we see that the cast on and bind off edges look the same. This happens because professional designers are well aware of the fact that identical edges instantly elevate the look of the knitted item.

In most cases, the edges are quite simple because designers are constrained by the limitations of knitting machines.

As hand-knitters, we are limited only by our imagination and the number of cast on and bind off methods that we are aware of.

This book gives you a selection of those methods to help you choose the best way to cast on and bind off stitches of your projects knowing that the edges will be identical just as they are in upscale knitwear.

We'll start by discussing the most basic pair of matching cast ons and bind offs—methods that are not flashy, but give our projects the subtle vibe of a well-finished garments.

In the second section of this book, we'll see how we can make our edges more prominent by adding different kinds of i-cords—regular i-cord, purled i-cord and a skinnier variation of the regular i-cord that adds a lovely three-faceted braid to the edges of our projects.

We'll see how all these methods can be applied to projects worked flat and the ones worked in the round.

If you need a quick reminder of the steps involved in performing each method, cut out the quick reference cards available at the end of each section, and keep those cards on hand as you add matching edges to your project.

Happy knitting, my friend!

Maryna

BASIC EDGES

CHAIN CAST ON AND SUSPENDED BIND OFF

STRETCH ★★★☆☆

DIFFICULTY ★★★☆☆

TOOLS

Let's start with a pair of methods that form a **neat chain of stitches** at the cast on and bind off edges of our projects.

While this look is created effortlessly when we bind off stitches by passing one stitch over the other, it is **a bit tricky** to achieve **when we cast on** a new set of stitches.

We can form a chain edge with two knitting needles and with the help of a **crochet hook**. The latter way is **easier and more straightforward**, so, in this book, we'll focus on that approach, because who needs unnecessary complications, right?

It is ok if you don't know how to crochet. This cast on method does not require any crocheting. We simply use a **crochet hook as a handy tool,** and I'll guide you through each step of the process with **close-up photos and tips** that will help you to master this method without any issues.

The edge formed by this cast on method is **fairly loose**. That's why it is better to choose a crochet hook that is **one or two sizes smaller** than the size of the knitting needles you are using to make the project.

CHAIN CAST ON WORKED FLAT

STEP 1

Make a **slip knot** and place it on the crochet hook.

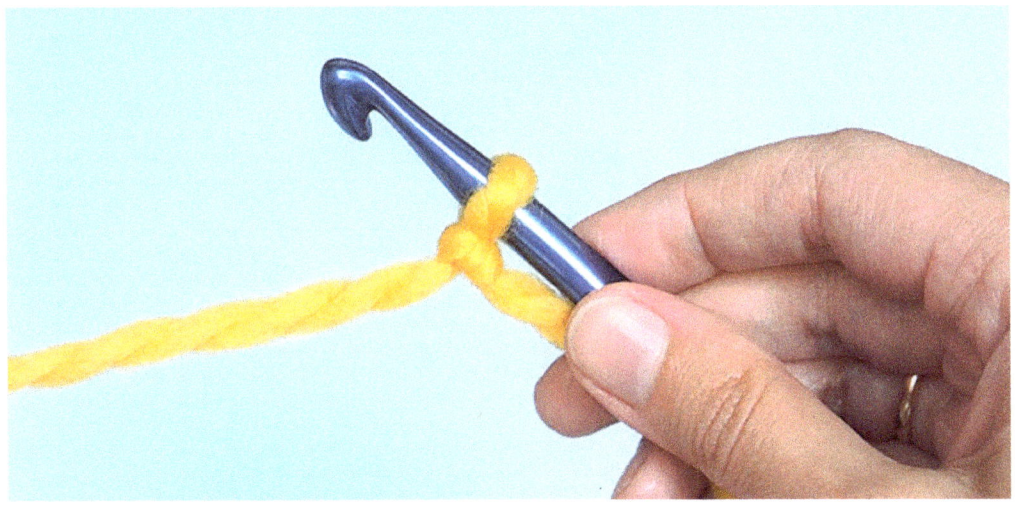

STEP 2

Align a knitting needle with the crochet hook so that the working **yarn is at the back** of the needle. Turn the crochet hook so that its **"nose" is facing you**. Hold the needle, the yarn tail, and the crochet hook in your left hand.

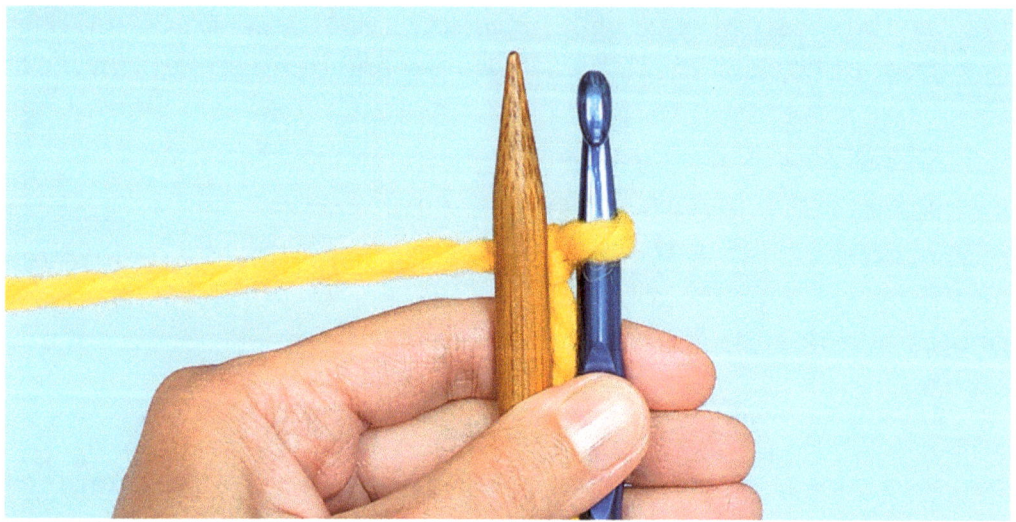

STEP 3

Take the working yarn in your right hand and move it **counter clockwise** around the top of the needle and the front of the crochet hook to wrap the yarn around them from back to front. Keep the **yarn wrap above the stitch** sitting on the crochet hook.

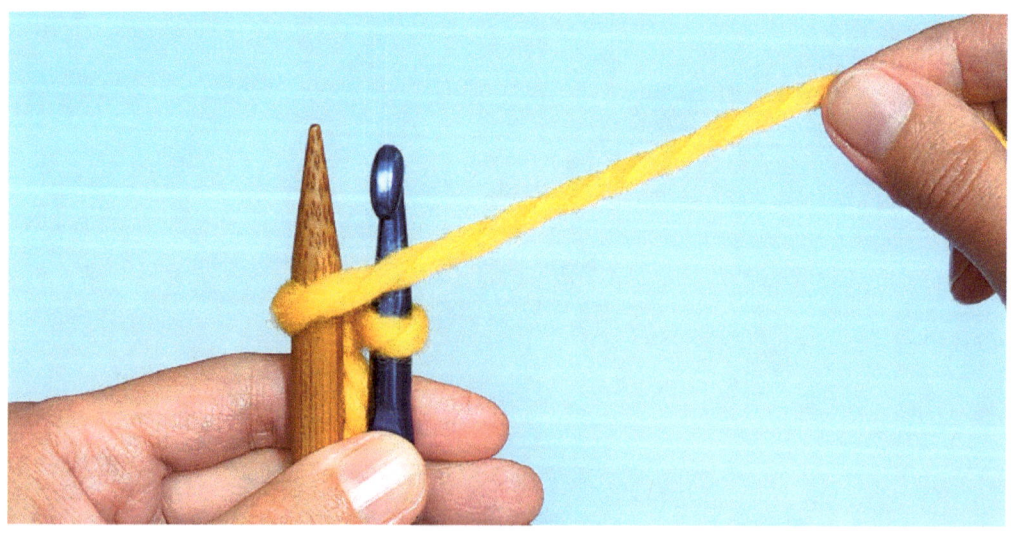

STEP 4

Take the crochet hook **in your right hand** and hold it together with the working yarn. Hold the knitting needle and the yarn tail in your left hand.

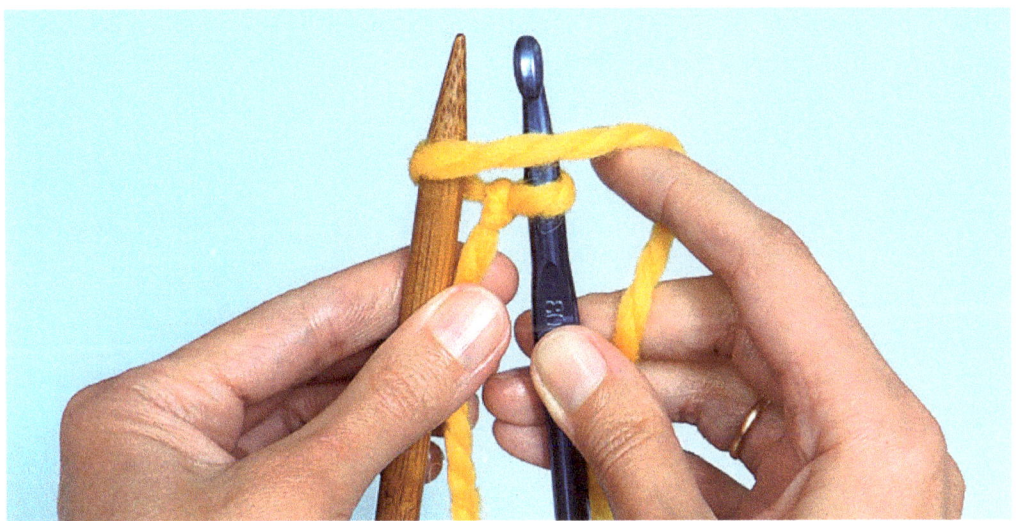

STEP 5

Twist the hook a bit so that its **"nose" catches the yarn wrap**. Then move the crochet hook down to **push the wrap through the stitch,** creating a new stitch on the knitting needle.

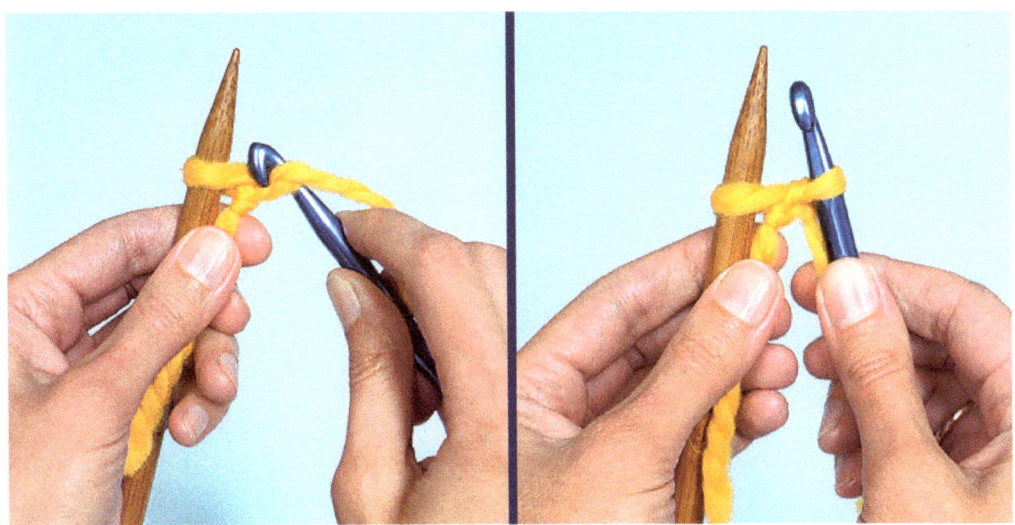

To make it easier for the hook to "dive" into the stitch, **pull the bottom of the stitch down,** opening the loop a bit more.

Repeat steps 2 through 5 until the number of stitches on the knitting needle equals the number of stitches that you need for the project **minus one stitch**. For example, to make a swatch worked on 10 stitches, I stop when I have 9 stitches on the knitting needle and one stitch on the crochet hook.

Insert the tip of the knitting needle **from right to left** into the stitch on the hook and ease the crochet hook out, leaving that stitch on the needle.

The easiest way to do it is to **stretch the last stitch** before you move it to the knitting needle, then pull the working yarn to tighten this stitch.

Now that we have the number of **stitches we need for the project**, we are ready to work the first row.

This cast on edge is **fully reversible**. It will look nice no matter whether the first row of your project is a right-side or a wrong-side row.

CHAIN CAST ON WORKED IN THE ROUND

Use the **same five steps** discussed above to cast on the stitches that you need for your project.

Arrange the stitches **for working in the round** using your favourite way to make seamless projects (double-pointed or circular needles).

Once you make sure the **edge is not twisted**, join the stitches into a circle by **passing the last stitch over the first one**, or simply start working the first round of your project.

An edge formed by the chain cast on **looks a lot like** an edge we see after we bind off stitches using the **regular "knit two, pass one over the other" method**. We have the same chain of stitches at the edge, but the **tension is different**—regular bind off is quite a bit tighter.

To make a bind off edge **that matches both the look and the density** of the chain cast on, we need to use a looser and more elastic variation of the regular bind off—the **suspended bind off**.

We'll use a **simple trick** that lets the humble regular bind off shine on **necklines, sock cuffs** and pretty much any other part of any other project.

SUSPENDED BIND OFF WORKED FLAT

Start by working **two stitches** one by one.

If your project is in garter stitch or a stockinette-based stitch pattern, or **if you don't need to bind off "in pattern"**, knit these stitches.

If you work in ribbing, or any other stitch pattern built by knits and purls, **knit the stitches that look like knits, and purl the ones that look like purls**. This way, you will bind off the stitches "in pattern".

My swatch is worked in **"knit 1, purl 1" ribbing**, so I knitted the first stitch and purled the next one.

The **three steps** that form this type of bind off edge **differ** depending on the type of stitch that is now the **first stitch on the left needle**.

If you are not binding off stitches "in pattern," bind off all stitches **as if they were knits**.

IF THE FIRST STITCH ON THE LEFT NEEDLE IS A KNIT

STEP 1

Bring the working **yarn to the back** of the work.

STEP 2

Insert the tip of the left needle **from left to right** into the **second stitch** on the right needle, and **pass this stitch over the first stitch** from the tip of the right needle.

Don't drop either of these stitches! This is the trick that makes all the difference. We keep the stitch-that-was-passed-over on the left needle. **This stitch is "suspended"**.

STEP 3

Even though the "suspended" stitch is still sitting on the left needle, we are going to **ignore it for now.**

Insert the right needle **from left to right** into the **stitch that is next** to the "suspended" stitch.

Wrap the tip of the right needle with the working yarn and pull this wrap through to **knit this stitch**.

Slip both the "just-knitted" and the "suspended" stitches **off the left needle**.

IF THE FIRST STITCH ON THE LEFT NEEDLE IS A PURL

STEP 1

Bring the working **yarn to the front** of the work.

STEP 2

Pass the second stitch from the tip of the right needle over the first one, but **don't drop the "passed-over" stitch** off the left needle yet. This is the "suspended" stitch that makes the edge looser and more elastic.

STEP 3

With the "suspended" stitch still on the left needle, **insert the right needle** from right to left **into the next stitch** on the left needle. Do this in such a way that the **right needle** stays **in front of the "suspended" stitch** and at the back of the working yarn.

Wrap the tip of the right needle with the working yarn, and pull this wrap through to **purl this stitch**. It could feel **a bit unusual** to pull a new stitch from between two stitches, but it is **not difficult at all**.

Slip both stitches **off the left needle**.

Repeat steps 1-3 until you bind off all stitches and there are only **two stitches** sitting **on the right needle**.

LAST STEP

Pass the second of these stitches over the first one and **off the right needle**, just as we do when we use the regular bind off method.

Cut the yarn, pass the tail **through the last stitch**, and pull tight to secure.

The **structure of an edge** formed by this type of bind off is **exactly the same** as the structure of an edge formed by the **regular bind off** method, but because we "suspend" each stitch we **keep it from tightening** as we work the next stitch.

This simple move **adds elasticity** to the edge and makes the chain of stitches **look exactly the same** as the stitches formed by the chain cast on method (page 11).

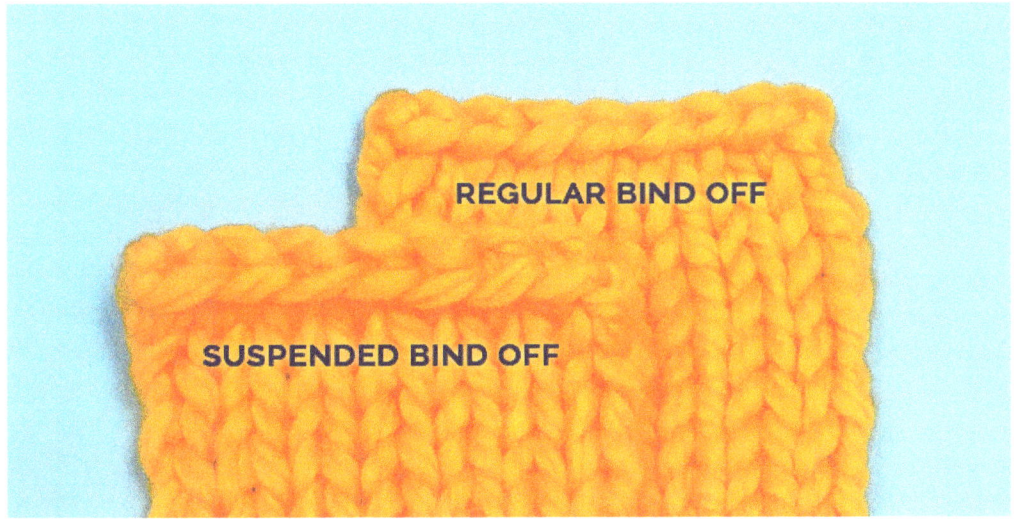

SUSPENDED BIND OFF WORKED IN THE ROUND

If you bind off stitches of a **seamless project**, follow **steps 1 through 3** described above until you bind off all stitches. You can bind off all stitches "in pattern", or choose an easier route and bind them off as knits.

No matter which approach you take, you will end up with an **unsightly gap** between the first and the last bound off stitches.

Don't worry – we can easily fix this gap in **two simple steps**.

FIXING THE GAP

When you finish binding off stitches, cut the yarn leaving a **tail around 15 cm / 6" long**. Thread this tail into a wool needle.

STEP 1

With the right side of the work facing you, insert the wool needle from front to back under **both legs of the first bound off stitch.**

Pull the yarn through, but don't pull it too tight. The strand between the last and the first stitches should be **as long as one leg of any other stitch** that forms the bind off edge.

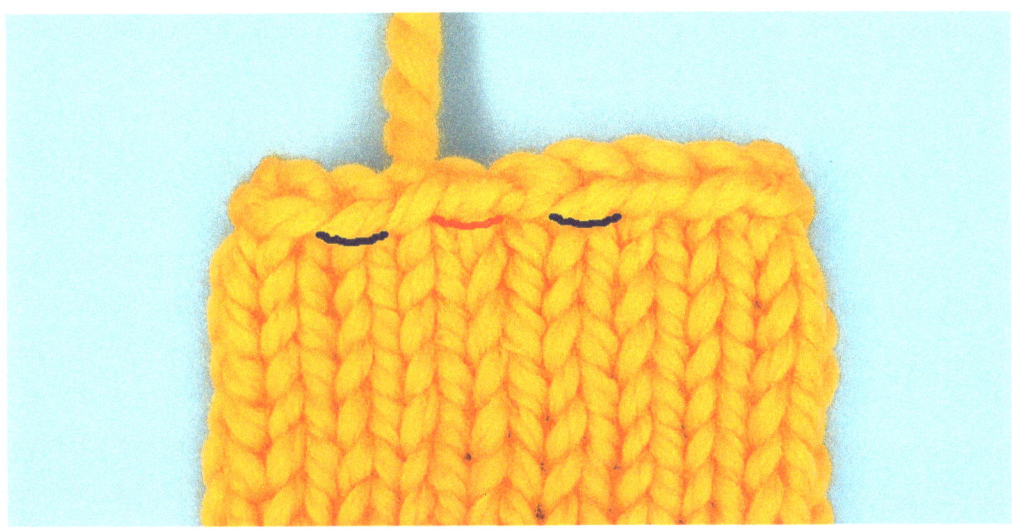

STEP 2

Now insert the wool needle from front to back **under the right leg of the last bound off stitch**.

Pull the yarn through so that **both strands** that join the first and the last stitches **are of the same length**.

Secure the yarn and enjoy the **perfectly seamless look** of the bind off edge.

As we have the **tail in the wool needle** already, it makes sense to **weave it in** on the wrong side of the work, or along the bind off edge if the project is reversible.

***TIP:** To add a lovely chain of stitches to **all four edges** of a project worked flat, **knit the first stitch** of every row **through the back loop** and **slip the last stitch** of every row purlwise with the yarn at the front of the work,*

ROLLED CAST ON AND ROLLED BIND OFF

STRETCH ★★★★☆

DIFFICULTY ★★★☆☆

TOOLS

Let's take the basic chain-looking edge up a notch and turn it into a **tiny roll** that is less subtle and **more elastic**. This cute little roll is formed by a few rows or rounds of stockinette stitch.

We don't need to do anything special to make it roll. The **natural properties of stockinette** take care of that for us.

This edge adds a **beautiful accent** to projects made in ribbing, seed stitch, cables, lace, and other **textured stitch patterns**, but not to stockinette stitch. We can't highlight stockinette stitch with a piece of stockinette stitch, right?

ROLLED CAST ON WORKED FLAT

STEP 1

Use the **chain cast on** explained on page 11 to cast on the number of stitches you need for your project.

STEP 2

Purl all stitches in the first row.

STEP 3

Knit all stitches in the next row.

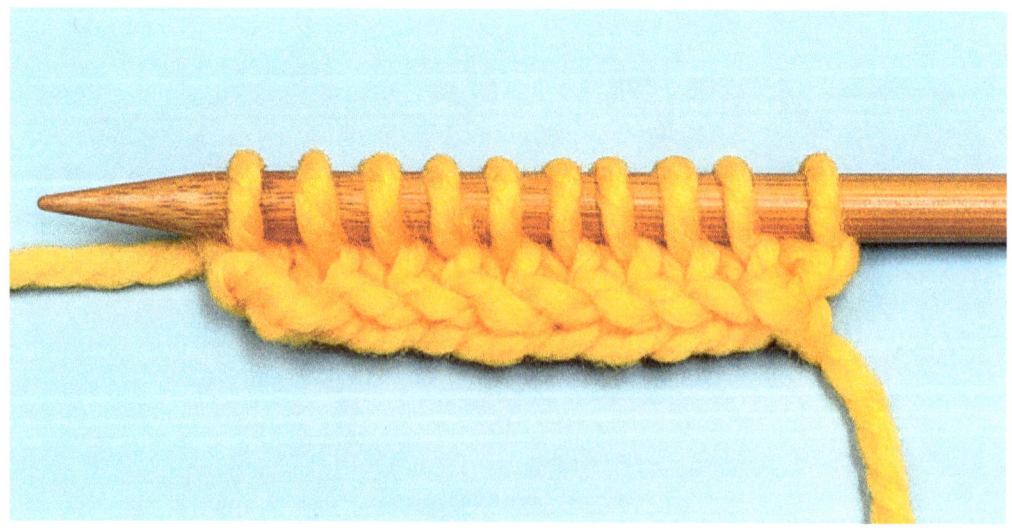

STEP 4

Purl all stitches again in what is **the last row** of this edging.

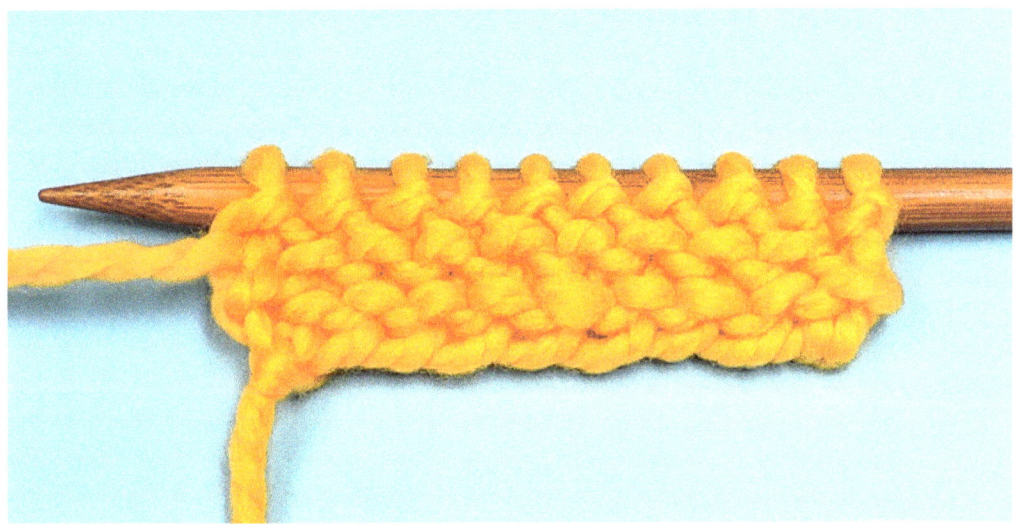

Then **work in the main pattern** of your project starting with a **right-side row**. My swatch is made in ribbing, so I alternated knit and purl stitches throughout each row.

Once you make a few rows you will notice that the **three rows of stockinette** stitch at the very bottom of the project **curl up**, forming a delicate roll made of purl "bumps".

ROLLED CAST ON WORKED IN THE ROUND

When we add this edge to a **seamless project**, the process is even **easier**.

We use the **chain cast on** method (page 11) to get the initial set of stitches on the needles. Then we arrange these stitches **for working in the round** and join them in a circle by passing the last stitch over the first one. Make sure the cast on **edge is not twisted** around the needles.

Once this step is done, we simply **knit all stitches** in every round for the first **three rounds**.

Then we are ready to **move on to the main pattern** of the project. This time, I will use the seed stitch (known as the "moss stitch" in the UK) to show you how lovely this edge looks next to a textured stitch pattern.

Because the very bottom of the project is now formed by a few rounds of rolled knitted fabric, the edge is **more elastic** and has a **more defined look**.

This is **the easiest way** to add a "bumpy" roll to a project edge. We'll talk about another way to get a similar look a bit later, when we discuss the **purled i-cord** cast on and bind off duo, but for now, let's see how we can form the same rolled edge when it is time to bind off stitches.

ROLLED BIND OFF WORKED FLAT

Because this edging **rolls towards the right side** of the fabric, it is important to start this bind off after you work the **last wrong-side row** of the project.

STEP 1

With the **right side of the fabric facing you**, knit all stitches for one row.

STEP 2

Knit all stitches in the next row.

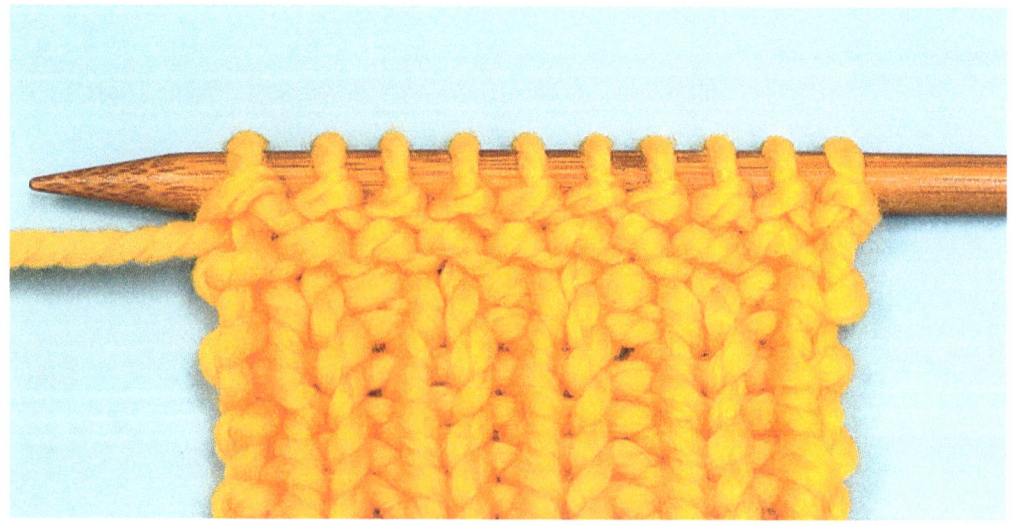

STEP 3

Use the **suspended bind off** method (page 16) to bind off all stitches as knits.

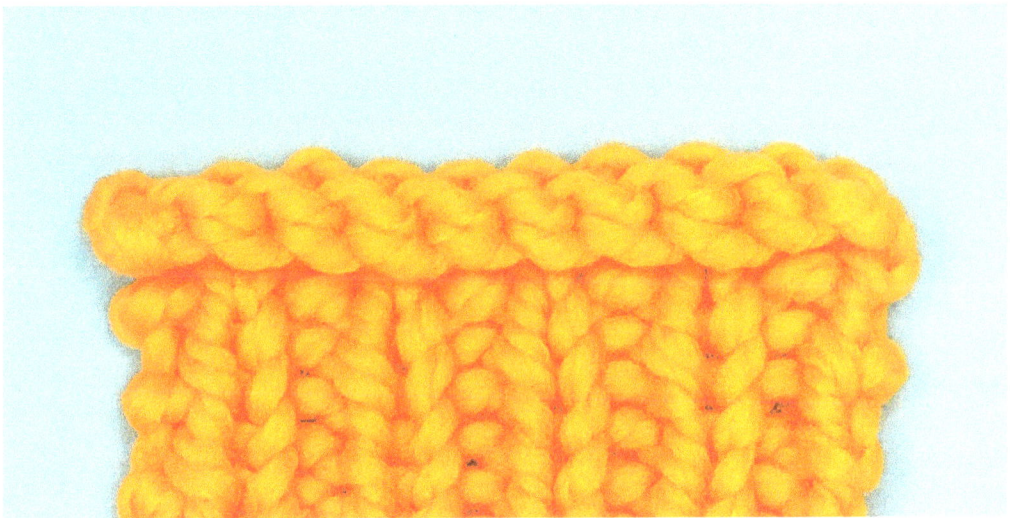

ROLLED BIND OFF WORKED IN THE ROUND

When we use this method to bind off stitches of a **seamless project**, we start by **knitting all stitches** in every round for **two rounds**.

Then we use the **suspended bind off** method (page 16) to form an elastic chain of stitches at the very edge of the roll, and we **close the gap** between the first and the last bound off stitches by following the steps explained in the **"Fixing the Gap"** segment on page 24.

Even though we have worked **only two rows or rounds** in stockinette stitch, the roll formed at the bind off edge is **identical** to the one formed by the rolled cast on method. This happens because the suspended bind off itself **adds a line of stitches** to the project.

TUCK CAST ON AND TUCK BIND OFF

STRETCH ★★★☆☆

DIFFICULTY ★★★★☆

TOOLS

The last pair of basic cast on and bind off methods discussed in this book is **not basic at all**. The edges formed by this duo look very much like an **embossed stockinette stitch**, but it is only a disguise.

In reality, these edges are "stockinette trainers". They **tame the infamous stockinette curl** and keep edges flat **without drastically changing the look** of this stitch pattern.

Of course, we can easily keep the edges of stockinette fabric flat when we **add a border** in a non-curling stitch pattern like garter stitch, seed stitch, or ribbing, but that **border will add a different texture** to our project.

When we want to preserve the **sleek look of stockinette** stitch, the tuck cast on and bind off methods are **invaluable**.

TUCK CAST ON WORKED FLAT

First, we use the **chain cast on** method described on page 11 to cast on the number of stitches that you need for your project.

Next, we **make a narrow band that will form a tuck**. This part is **very easy**. We simply purl all stitches in the first row, knit all stitches in the next row and, finally, purl all stitches again in the last row of the band.

Turn the work so that the **knit side of the fabric is facing you**.

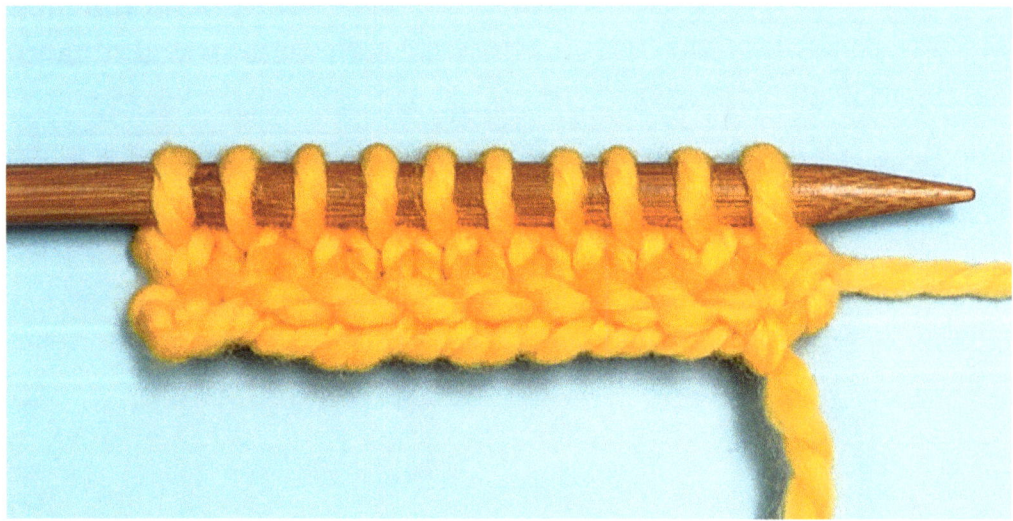

Rotate the fabric around the knitting needle so that the **cast on edge is at the top** of the needle, and the working **yarn is at the right-hand side** of the fabric. Take an empty knitting needle in your right hand.

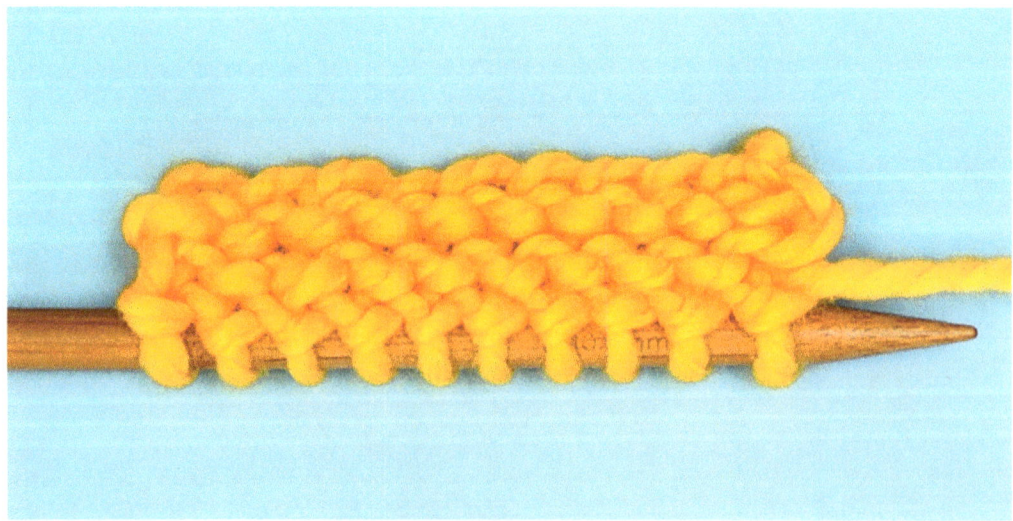

Now we are ready to **work the "tuck row"**—a row where we use our three-row band to form a "curl-preventing" tuck. We do it by **picking up a strand from the first row** of the fabric and **knitting it together** with the corresponding stitch on the left needle.

The way the fabric is arranged right now, the strands that we are going to pick up form **upward curves.** They look like **"smiles",** not like "arches".

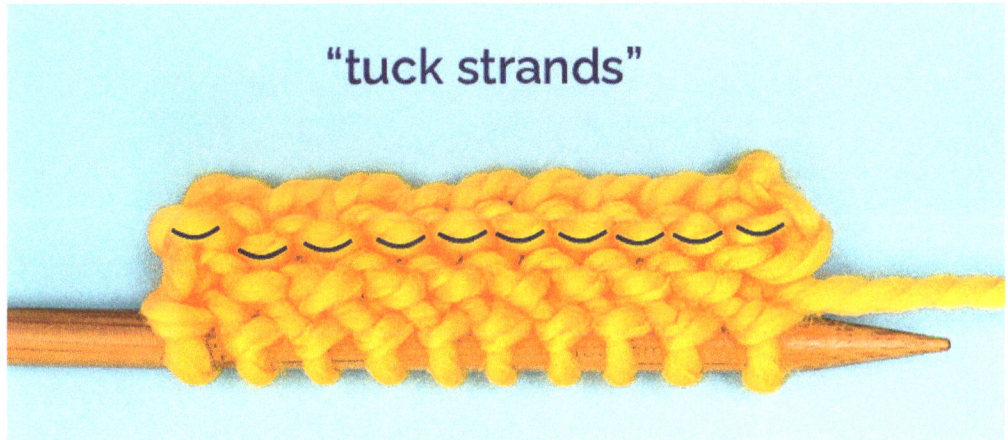

STEP 1

Insert the tip of the right needle **from the top down** under the "tuck strand" that **corresponds to the first stitch** on the left needle.

With the cast on edge at the top of the knitting needle, this strand will be the **top upward curve ("smile") above the first stitch** from the tip of the left needle.

STEP 2

Stretch this strand a bit and **place it on the left needle**. Do it purlwise, **without twisting** the strand.

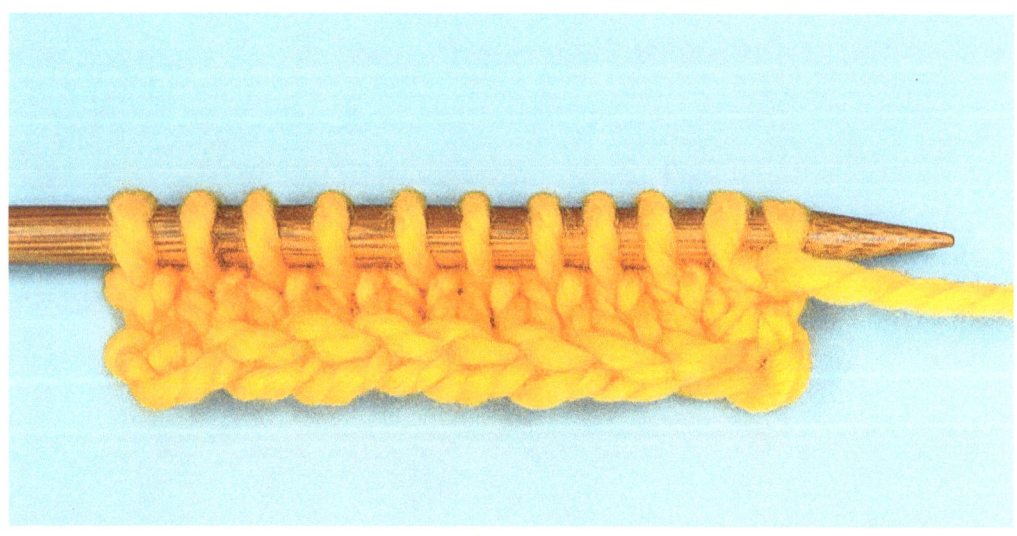

STEP 3

Knit the first stitch from the tip of the left needle **together with the picked-up strand**.

Repeat **these three steps** until you pick up all "tuck strands" and knit them together with the corresponding stitches sitting on the left needle. Make sure the working **yarn does not get caught** between the stitch and the picked-up strand.

The cast on edge is formed and now we can **work in the main pattern of the project**

Note that the **next row will be a wrong-side row**, so follow the pattern instructions for a wrong-side row. If you work in stockinette stitch, purl all stitches.

TUCK CAST ON WORKED IN THE ROUND

To add this edge to a **seamless project**, use the **chain cast on** method (page 11) to cast on the number of stitches you need for your project.

Arrange the stitches **for working in the round**. You can do this by using **one long circular needle** and the magic loop method, or by using **any other setup** that allows us to make seamless projects.

If you prefer to **join stitches in a circle**, you can do it by passing the last stitch over the first one. Or, you can simply **start working the first round** right away. In either case, make sure the **stitches are not twisted** around the needles.

Knit all stitches in every round for **three rounds**. This way, you'll **make a band** that will form the tuck at the bottom of the cast on edge.

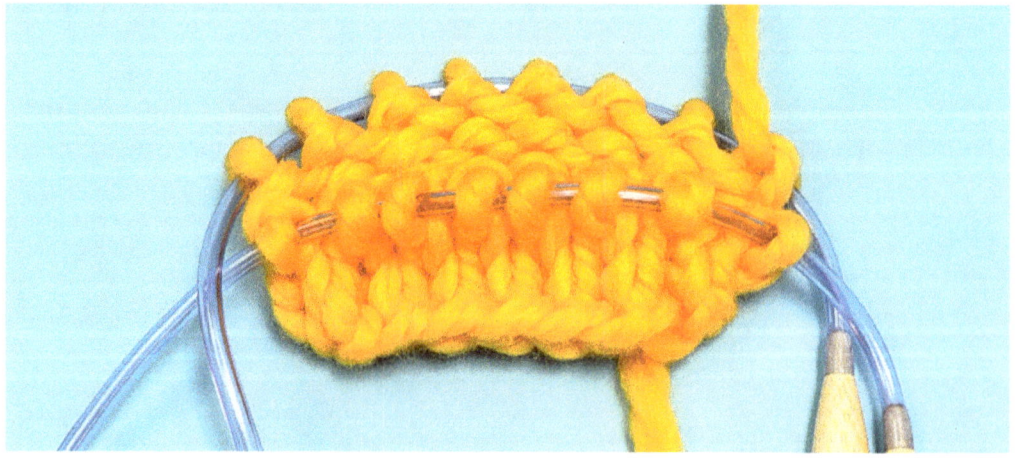

The next round will be the **"tuck-forming"** one. Turn the fabric **inside out** so that the cast on edge is at the top.

Then **repeat the same three steps** that we followed when we formed a tuck at the bottom of a piece worked flat—pick up the "smile" strand that is **above the first stitch** on the left needle, place that strand on the left needle, and **knit it together** with the first stitch.

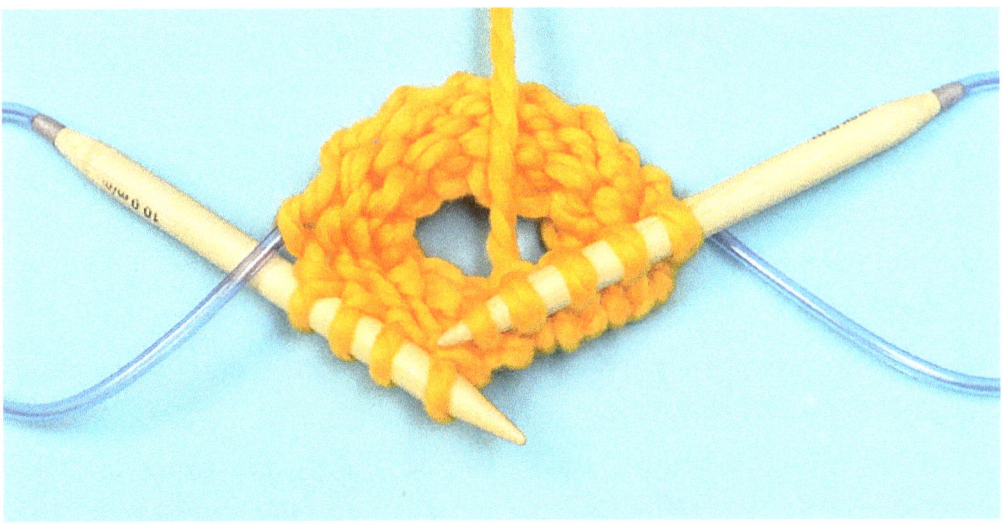

BASIC EDGES | 45

Do it until you **knit all "tuck strands"** together with the corresponding stitches.

Now **work in the main pattern** of your project. If it is stockinette stitch, knit all stitches in every round.

The edge formed by this cast on method is **quite stretchy**. That makes it **perfect for any project**, from hats and sweaters to mittens and loose top-down socks.

This edge will keep the stockinette stitch fabric from curling up, **especially after you block** your project.

To form an **identical edge** at the other end of the fabric, we should use the tuck bind off method.

MATCHING CAST ONS & BIND OFFS

TUCK BIND OFF WORKED FLAT

When you are ready to bind off stitches of your project, work in stockinette stitch **for three rows** to form the "tuck band".

Because this bind off is worked **in a right-side row**, the first row of stockinette stitch should be a **wrong-side row**.

To make the "tuck band" turn the project so that the **wrong side of the work is facing you**. Purl all stitches in one row, then knit all stitches in the next row and purl all stitches in the row after that. Turn your work and you will **face the right side** of the fabric.

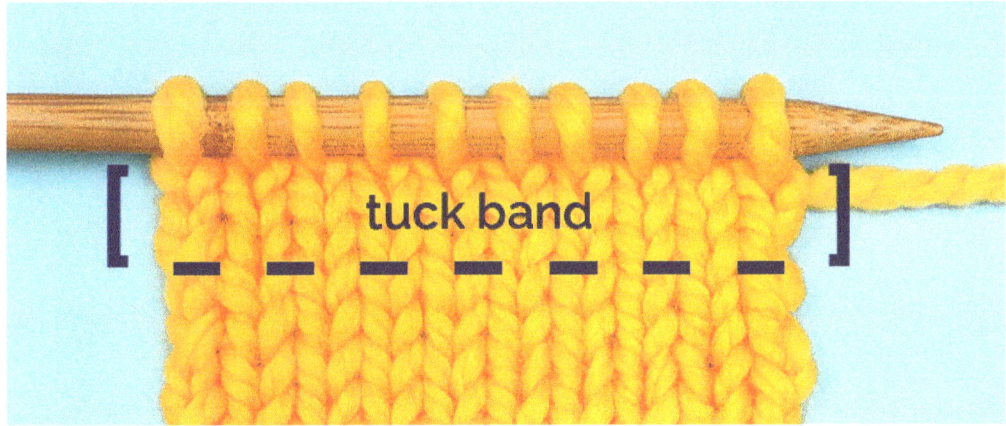

The next row is a **"tuck row"**. Rotate the fabric around the needle so that the **wrong side** of at least three rows of the fabric **shows at the top** of the knitting needle. Keep the working **yarn at the right** edge of the project.

Find the **third "smile" at the top of the first stitch** on the left needle. The first "smile" will be the "bump" right above the stitch sitting on the needle. The second "smile" will be right above that "bump", and the strand that we are looking for is **above that second "smile"**.

Once you find the first "tuck strand", it will be **easy to find the rest of them** because they are all in the same line of stitches.

STEP 1

Insert the right needle **from the top down** under the "tuck strand" that is **above the first stitch** on the left needle.

STEP 2

Place this strand **purlwise** on the tip of the left needle.

STEP 3

Knit the picked-up strand **together with the first stitch** on the left needle.

STEP 4

Work steps 1, 2, and 3 **one more time**.

STEP 5

Pass the second stitch from the tip of the right needle over the first one and off the needle to **bind off one stitch**.

Repeat **steps 4 and 5** over and over again until you bind off all stitches. To match the elasticity of the edge formed by the tuck cast on method, **keep the bind off edge loose**.

TUCK BIND OFF WORKED IN THE ROUND

Just as we did when we used this method to bind off stitches of a project worked flat, start by working **three rounds in the stockinette stitch** pattern.

For seamless projects, this means **knitting all stitches in every round** for three rounds.

Rotate the fabric around the needles **to see the wrong side** of the last three rounds showing above the needles.

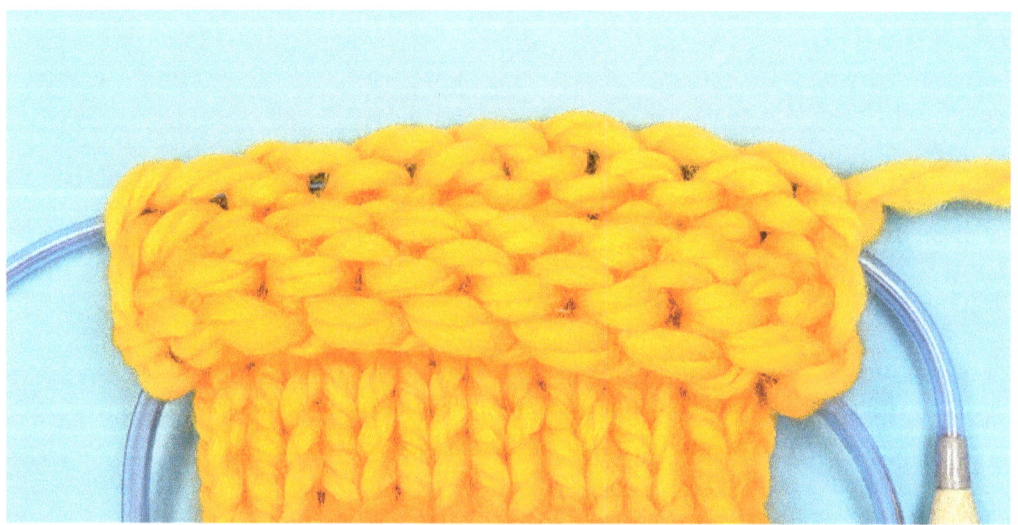

Work the **same five steps** that we followed when we bound off stitches of a project worked flat—pick up the third "smile" above the first stitch on the left needle, place that strand on the needle, and knit it together with the corresponding stitch. Then do it **one more time**.

Once you have two stitches on the right needle, **bind off one stitch**.

BASIC EDGES | 53

Repeat this process **until you bind off all stitches**. To make the edge fully seamless, use the trick described on page 24 to **join the first and the last bound off stitches** into a perfect circle.

Don't tighten the stitches as you bind them off. The **edge should be quite loose** to match the stretch of the edge formed by the tuck cast on method.

Whether your project is worked flat or in the round, the bind off edge will **still look like stockinette** stitch, but with a slightly different texture. The **edge is thicker** and the fabric **does not tend to curl up** as easily. Block your project to leave the "stockinette curl" no chance.

Quick reference card

CHAIN CAST ON

Use a crochet hook that is **one or two sizes smaller** than the needles.

Make a slip knot, place it on the crochet hook, and align the hook with a knitting needle.

Move the yarn from the back of the needle to the front of the crochet hook.

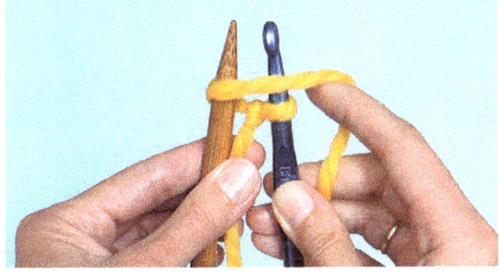

Hold the hook and the yarn in your right hand, and the needle and the yarn tail in your left hand.

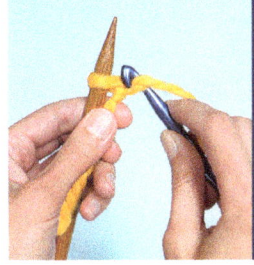

Move the hook down so that its "nose" catches the yarn and pushes it through the stitch.

Repeat these steps until you cast on the number of stitches you need minus one stitch.

Slip the last stitch knitwise from the crochet hook to the knitting needle.

BASIC EDGES | 55

Quick reference card

SUSPENDED BIND OFF

Work two stitches one by one (knit the knits and purl the purls).

FOR A KNIT STITCH: With yarn at back, pass the second stitch on the right needle over the first one.

With the "suspended" stitch still on the left needle, knit one stitch.

Slip both the "just-knitted" and the "suspended" stitches off the left needle.

FOR A PURL STITCH: With yarn in front, pass the second stitch on the right needle over the first one.

With the "suspended" stitch still on the left needle, purl one stitch.

Slip the "just-purled" and the "suspended" stitches off the needle.

Quick reference card

ROLLED CAST ON

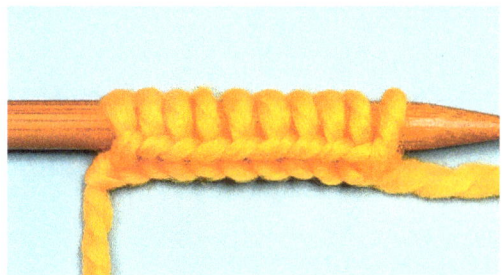

Use the chain cast on method to cast on the number of stitches you need.

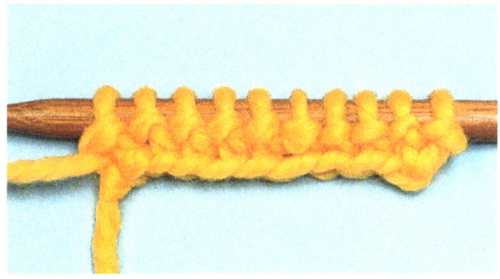

Purl all stitches in the first row..

Knit all stitches in the next row.

Purl all stitches again in what is the last row of the edging.

Then work the first right-side row of your project.

When working in the round, knit all stitches for three rounds.

BASIC EDGES | 57

Quick reference card

ROLLED BIND OFF

With the right side of the fabric facing you, knit all stitches for one row.

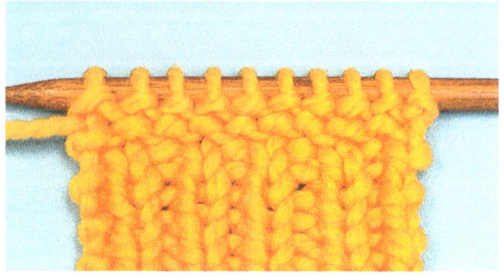

Purl all stitches in the next row.

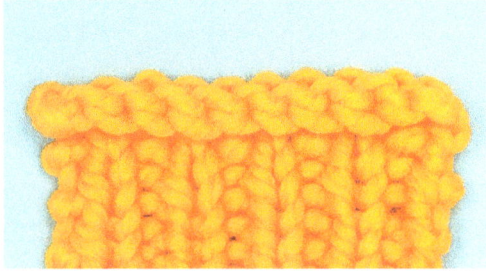

Use the suspended bind off method to bind off all stitches as knits.

When working in the round, knit all stitches in every round for two rounds before you bind off all stitches using the suspended bind off method.

Quick reference card
TUCK CAST ON

Use chain cast on to cast on the number of stitches you need.

Make the "tuck band"—purl all stitches in row 1, knit them in row 2, and purl them again in row 3.

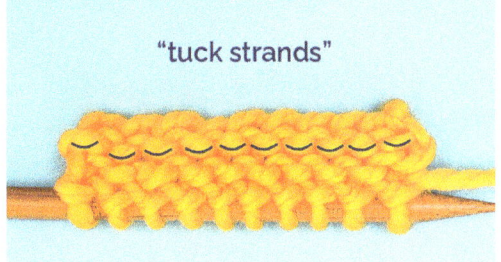

Rotate the fabric around the needle and find the "tuck strands" in the first row of the band.

Insert the right needle from the top down under the "tuck strand" that corresponds to the first stitch.

Place this strand purlwise on the tip of the left needle.

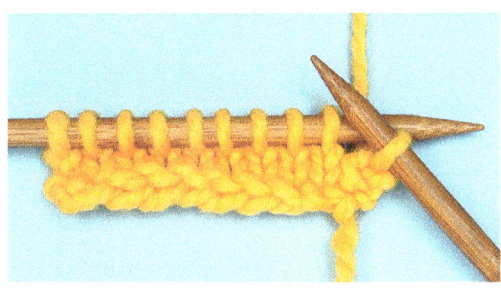

Knit the first stitch on the left needle together with the picked-up strand.

Repeat these steps until you knit all "tuck strands" together with the corresponding stitches

BASIC EDGES | 59

Quick reference card

TUCK BIND OFF

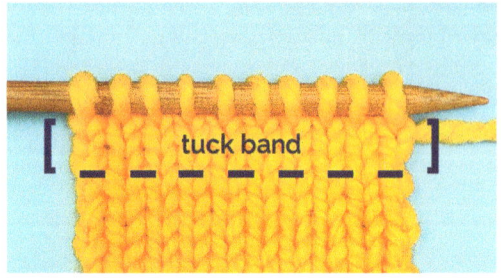

With the wrong side facing you, purl all stitches in row 1, knit them in row 2, and purl them in row 3.

Rotate the fabric around the needle and find the "tuck strands" in the first row of the tuck band.

STEP 1: Insert the right needle under the "tuck strand" that corresponds to the first stitch.

STEP 2: Place this strand purlwise on the tip of the left needle.

STEP 3: Knit the first stitch on the left needle together with the picked-up strand.

Repeat steps 1-3 one more time, then pass the second stitch on the right needle over the first one.

Repeat until you bind off all stitches.

I-CORD EDGES

I-CORD CAST ON AND I-CORD BIND OFF

STRETCH ★★☆☆☆

DIFFICULTY ★★★☆☆

TOOLS

We'll start this section of the book by discussing a way to make **cast on and bind off edges** that look as if they've been finished with an **applied i-cord**.

These edges have a polished look that is **identical on both sides of the fabric**. This makes them perfect for scarves, blankets, and other reversible projects.

The cast on method described in this chapter is an **improved version** of the classic i-cord cast on. A little tweak to this well-known technique helps us **avoid having a set of loose stitches** in the first row or round of the project.

I call this method a **"simplified i-cord cast on"** because it is indeed very simple. There are **only three steps** that are easy enough **even for absolute beginners**.

I-CORD CAST ON WORKED FLAT

We start by **casting on stitches of the i-cord**. It could be **three to five stitches**, but I find that a three-stitch version looks **neater and sleeker** than a wider i-cord. If you want to make a four or five-stitch i-cord, you can easily adjust the instructions in this tutorial.

As for the **cast on method** used to form those three (or more) stitches, use any one you like. I prefer to use a **slingshot version of the long-tail cast on** because it doesn't start with a rigid slip knot.

Arrange the work so that the tip of the needle and the working yarn are **at the right side**.

If you used the long-tail cast on method, turn the work. If you used the knitted or cable cast on method, you are all set to start adding more stitches to your needles.

STEP 1

Take the needle with the stitches in your left hand, and the other needle in your right hand. Place the right needle **on the working yarn** and bring the yarn **over that needle and to the back** of the work, making a **reverse yarn over**.

STEP 2

Knit the **stitches of the i-cord**. For my swatch, it means knitting three stitches, but if your i-cord is wider, knit four or five stitches.

The **very first stitch** that we cast on by making a reverse yarn over is **usually loose**. This happens because we don't have any fabric yet to anchor that first yarn over.

To tighten that stitch, **stop after you knit the first stitch** of the i-cord and **pull the yarn** a bit.

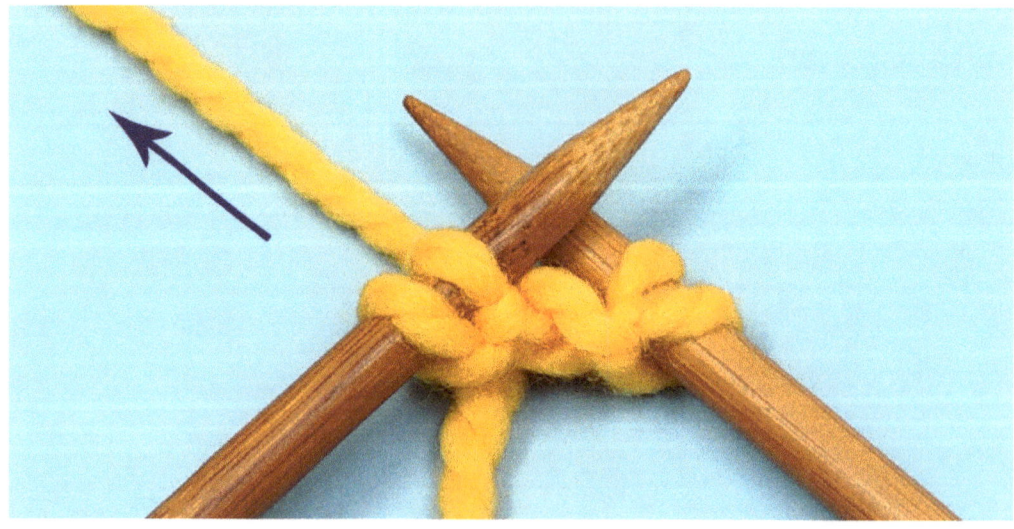

You will only need to **do this once**. Now that the needles are well-balanced, **the rest of the stitches** we cast on will be of the **right size**.

STEP 3

Insert the tip of the left needle **from left to right** into the first stitch on the right needle and ease the right needle out, **slipping that stitch** to the left needle.

Do it again and again until you **slip all stitches of the i-cord** to the left needle.

Repeat these three steps until you cast on the number of stitches that you need for your project **minus one stitch**. This number **does not include** the stitches of the i-cord.

Once you have the required number of stitches on your needles, **stop after you do step 3** (when the stitches of the i-cord are on the left needle and the stitches formed by reverse yarn overs are on the right needle).

For example, **to cast on eight stitches** for my swatch, I stop when I have **seven stitches on the right needle** and three stitches of the i-cord on the left needle.

LAST STEP

Knit the stitches of the i-cord **together**.

For my swatch this means knitting three stitches together, but **if your i-cord is wider,** you will need to knit four or five stitches together.

66 | MATCHING CAST ONS & BIND OFFS

Now, the number of stitches on the right needle is the same as the number we need for the project. The cast on is finished and we are **ready to work the first row.**

ROW 1

The first row is a **wrong-side row**.

Turn the project and work all stitches according to the pattern instructions for a wrong-side row. For example, to work in stockinette stitch, **purl all stitches** in this row.

As we do with any i-cord we make, **pull the i-cord edge** sideways to properly **distribute the yarn** between the stitches. You can do it after you work a few rows, or after the first row.

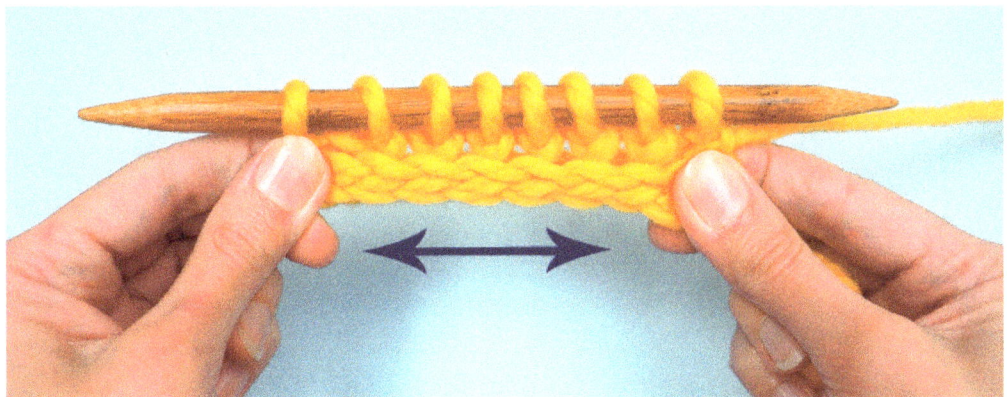

You will see that this simple action not only **evens out the edge**, but also makes the stitches of the first row **smaller and neater**.

I-CORD CAST ON WORKED IN THE ROUND

When we apply this method to a seamless project, the cast on itself is made in exactly **the same way** as the i-cord cast on worked flat.

There are only **two minor adjustments:** (a) the **yarn tail** that we leave before we cast on stitches should be **around 30 cm / 12" long**, and (b) we make reverse yarn overs until we cast on **all stitches** that we need for the project.

So, leave a medium-sized yarn tail and **cast on three to five stitches** depending on the width of the i-cord.

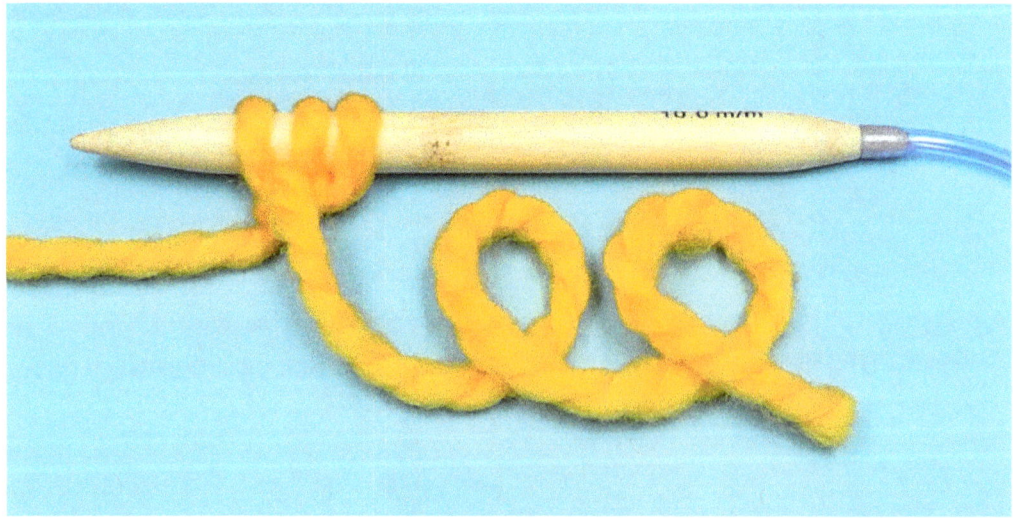

Arrange the work so that the **yarn is at the right side** of the stitches. Take the needle with the stitches in your left hand and an empty needle in your right hand.

Work the **same three steps** that we repeated when we used this cast on method on a swatch worked flat. Stop when you cast on the **number of stitches that you need** for your project (excluding the stitches of the i-cord).

For example, to cast on 20 stitches for my swatch, I stop when I have 20 stitches on the right needle and 3 stitches of the i-cord slipped to the left needle.

Slip the stitches of the i-cord **purlwise** from the left needle **to the right needle**.

Now comes the **tricky part**—joining the i-cord cast on edge in a circle. We want to do it seamlessly so that the **join is fully invisible**. This means **grafting** the stitches of the first row of the i-cord to the corresponding stitches of the last row of the i-cord.

To get ready for grafting, arrange the stitches for **working in the round**—divide them between **double-pointed needles**, divide them between **two circular needles**, spread them on **one short circular needle**, or split them in half if you use one long circular needle and the **magic loop** method.

No matter how you divide the stitches, **add the stitches of the i-cord** to the group of stitches that is the **closest to the tip of the right needle**.

For example, to work with the **magic loop** method I split the 20 stitches that I cast on **in half**, moved the first group of 10 stitches to the other side of a long circular needle, and separated it with a magic loop from the other group that includes 10 stitches of the cast on edge **plus 3 stitches of the i-cord**.

Arrange the cast on edge so that the **first row of the i-cord is at the left** side and the **live stitches of the i-cord are at the right** side. Make sure the **cast on edge is not twisted**.

Thread the yarn tail into a wool needle and move the **working yarn to the right** to keep it out of the way. To make it easier for you to see how this method works, I'll use a yarn tail in a contrasting colour.

STEP 1

Insert the wool needle **from back to front** into the **first stitch** from the tip of the right needle (it will be the first stitch at the left side of the i-cord).

Slip this stitch **off the needle** and pull the yarn through so that the strand between the ends of the i-cord is **as long as one leg of any stitch** that forms the i-cord.

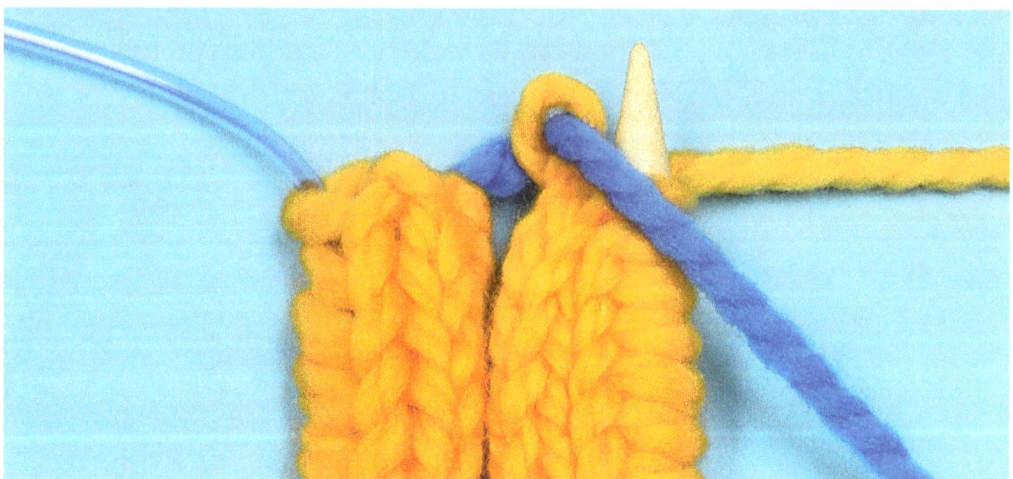

Because the working yarn is attached to this stitch, the stitch could **easily get loose**. Pull the working yarn a bit to adjust the size of the stitch, but **don't make it too tight**—it should be as big as the rest of the stitches.

STEP 2

Insert the wool needle **from right to left under both legs** of the first stitch at the right side of the first row of the i-cord. Because the **i-cord is upside down**, this stitch will look like an **inverted V**.

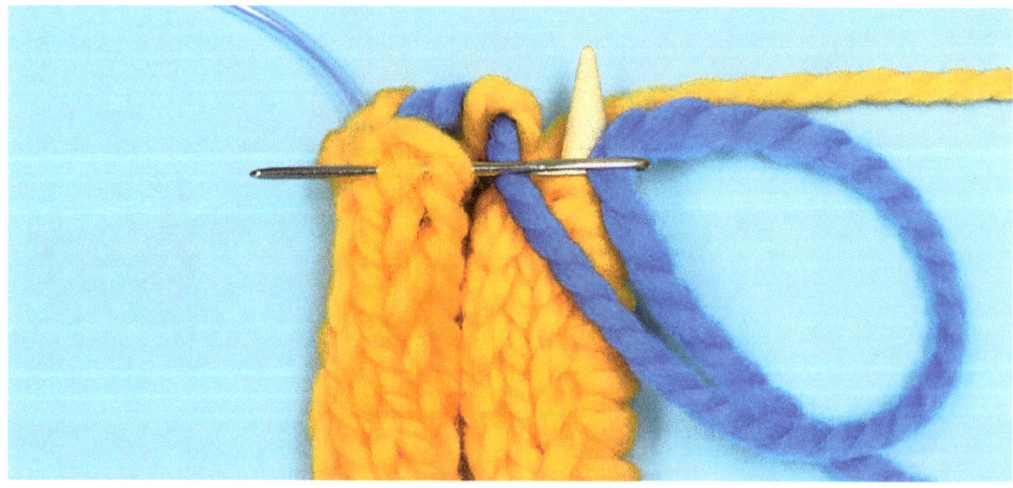

Pull the yarn through leaving a strand that is **as long as one leg of an average stitch** of the i-cord.

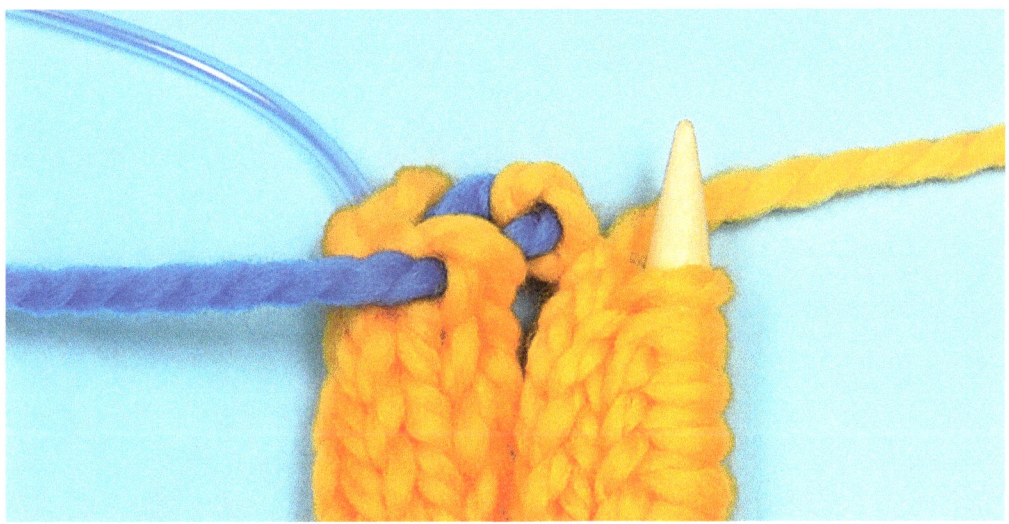

It is **very important** to keep every strand of the seam as long as one leg of an average stitch. This way, we'll **make the seam fully invisible**.

STEP 3

Insert the wool needle **from the top down** into the stitch that we slipped two steps ago, and **from back to front** into the first stitch from the tip of the right needle.

Slip this stitch off the knitting needle, **pull the yarn through,** and form another strand of the seam.

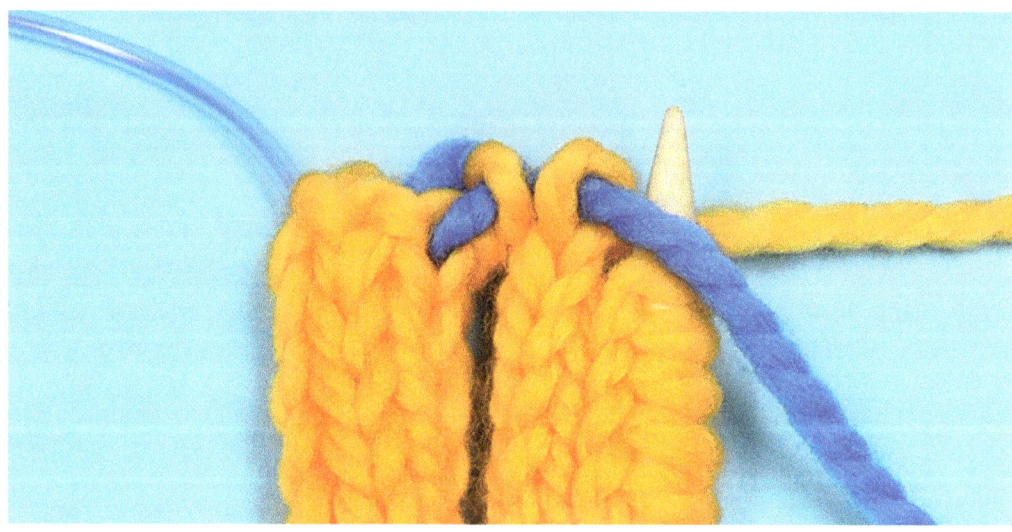

STEP 4

Insert the wool needle **from right to left** under two legs (another inverted V) of the **next stitch** in the first row of the i-cord.

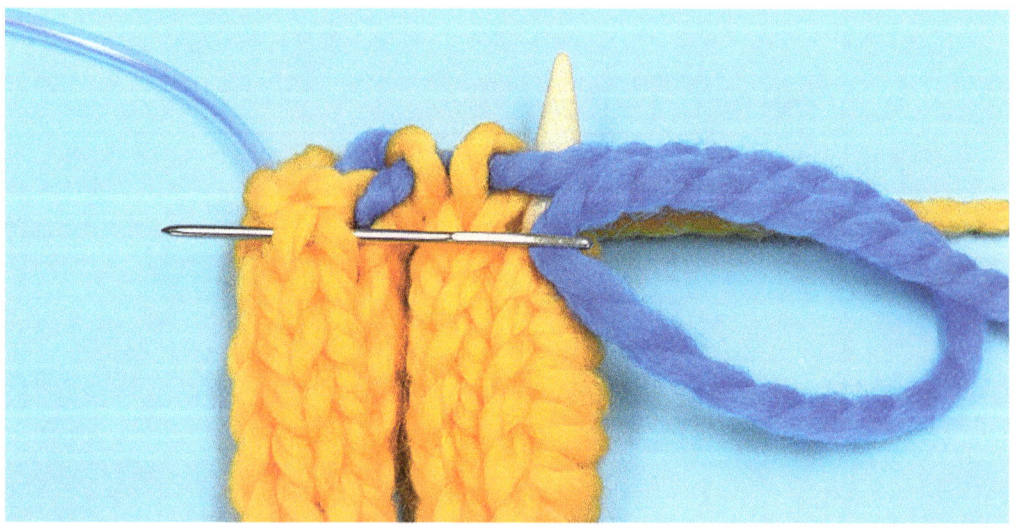

Pull the yarn through and **adjust the length of the strand**.

Repeat steps 3 and 4 until you **join all live stitches** of the i-cord to the corresponding stitches of the first row of the i-cord.

I-CORD EDGES | 75

LAST STEP

Insert the wool needle **from front to back** into the last live stitch of the i-cord and **from back to front** into the first stitch of the last row of the i-cord (the stitch that we slipped off the needle in step 1).

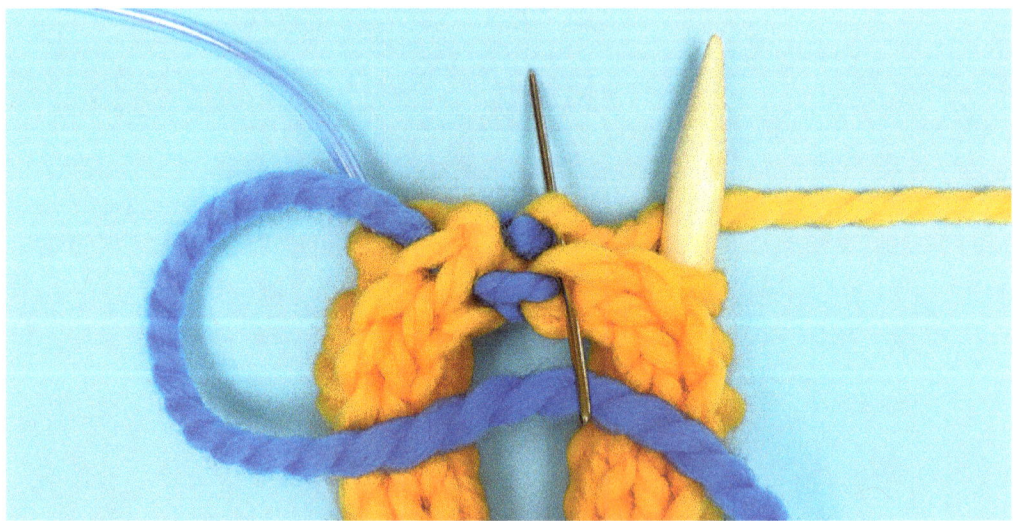

Pull the yarn through and **shape the last strand** of the seam.

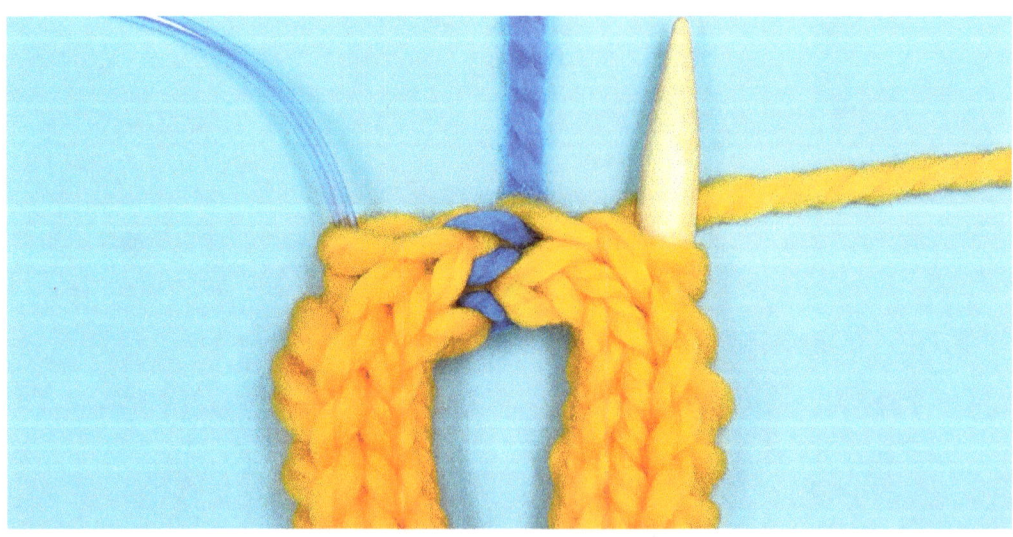

Secure the yarn and **hide the tail** inside the i-cord.

If the **yarn is thick**, you can skip the "secure the yarn" step to avoid forming a bulky knot. But if the **yarn is slippery**, it is **safer to secure the yarn** to make sure the stitches of the seam don't unravel when you wear this garment.

As you see, the seam we've just formed **blends perfectly with the i-cord**. This is why it is a good idea to **place a stitch marker** before we start to work the first round. The marker will be the only way to tell where the beginning of the round is.

In the first round, work according to the pattern of your choice, knitting and purling stitches as usual, **through the front loop**.

Because we cast on stitches by making reverse yarn overs, working them through the front loop will form a **neat line of twisted stitches** that will prop the i-cord and make it even more vivid.

The i-cord cast on is a perfect way to cast on stitches for scarves, blankets, shawls, sweaters, cardigans, bottom-up hats, and other projects that benefit from a **lovely well-finished edge** with a **moderate amount of stretch**.

Now let's take a look at a way to make a **bind off edge that is identical** to the edge formed by the i-cord cast on method.

I-CORD BIND OFF WORKED FLAT

We bind off stitches in a **right-side row**. When it is time to finish off your project, work the last wrong-side row and turn the work so that the **right side of the fabric is facing you** and the working **yarn is at the right-hand side** of the project.

The first thing that we do when we bind off stitches using this method is a bit counterintuitive—we **start by casting on a few extra stitches**. These are the stitches that will **form an i-cord** at the bind-off edge of the project.

To match an edge formed by the i-cord cast on method (page 62), the **number of stitches** that we cast on now should be **the same** as the number of stitches that we used to form an i-cord **at the cast on edge**.

Because I made a **three-stitch i-cord** at the cast on edge of my swatch, I am going to **cast on three stitches** before I bind off my stitches.

To make sure these additional stitches merge flawlessly with the stitches of the project, use the **knitted cast on** method.

First, insert the tip of the right needle **from left to right** into the first stitch on the left needle.

Wrap the right needle with the yarn the **same way as we do when we knit** a stitch.

Pull this wrap through the stitch to **form a new stitch**.

Place the newly-formed stitch on the left needle. Do it **purlwise**, without twisting the stitch.

Repeat these steps until you **cast on three or more stitches**, depending on the width of the i-cord you plan to make.

Cable cast on method is **also a good way** to cast on stitches for the future i-cord. If you like that method better than the knitted cast on, feel free to use it.

Now we are **all set** to form a beautiful bind off edge with an i-cord "topping".

STEP 1

Knit all stitches until you get **to the last stitch of the i-cord**. If your i-cord is worked on three stitches, knit two stitches.

If your i-cord is wider, knit three or four stitches.

STEP 2

Knit the next two stitches **together through the back loop**. These two are the last stitch of the i-cord and the first stitch of the fabric.

To knit them through the back loop, insert the tip of the right needle into both these stitches **from right to left**.

Wrap the right needle with the working yarn and **pull the wrap through**, forming a new stitch. Then slip the "worked" stitches off the left needle.

By knitting these stitches through the back loop, **we twist them**. This set of twisted stitches will **prop the i-cord** the same way as the set of reverse yarn overs props the i-cord at the edge formed by the i-cord cast on method. These little tweaks make the i-cords at both edges **more vivid** and our projects **more beautiful**.

STEP 3

Slip the stitches of the i-cord **one by one** back to the left needle. Do it **purlwise**. We don't need any more twisted stitches in this i-cord.

Repeat **these three steps** until you bind off all stitches of your project and there are **only stitches of the i-cord** sitting on your right needle.

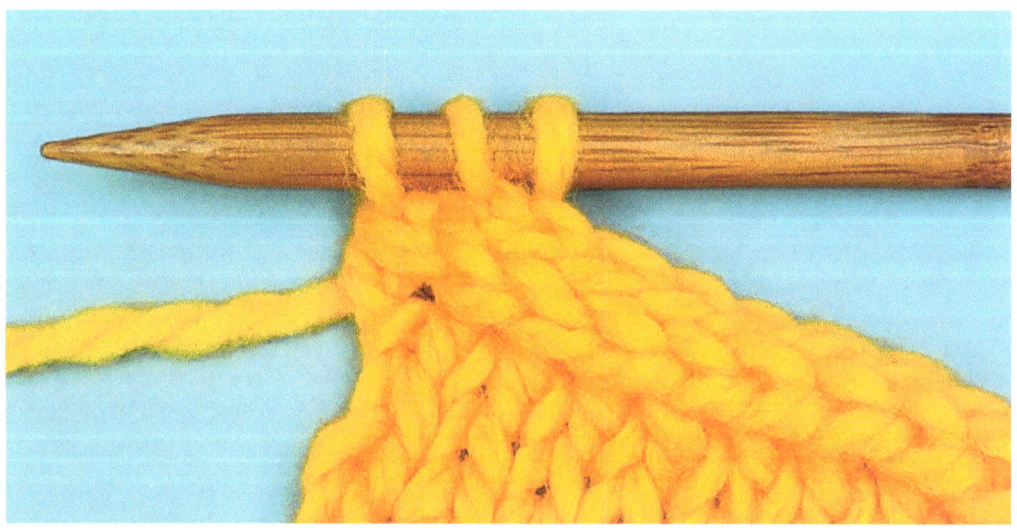

Cut the yarn leaving a **small tail** (10-15 cm / 4-6"). Thread this tail into a wool needle and run the wool needle **through the remaining stitches**.

Pull the yarn tail to **tighten the stitches** of the i-cord.

Then **secure the yarn** and hide the tail inside the i-cord.

As you see in the photo below, the edges formed by the i-cord cast on and bind off methods are **not only identical**, they are also **fully reversible**.

I-CORD BIND OFF WORKED IN THE ROUND

When we want to use the i-cord bind off method to finish off stitches of a **seamless project,** we follow the same process as we did when we used this method to bind off stitches of a project worked flat.

We start by **casting on three (or more) stitches** that will form the future i-cord.

Then we knit all stitches **to the last stitch of the i-cord**, knit the next two stitches **together through the back loop**, and return the stitches of the i-cord **back to the left needle**.

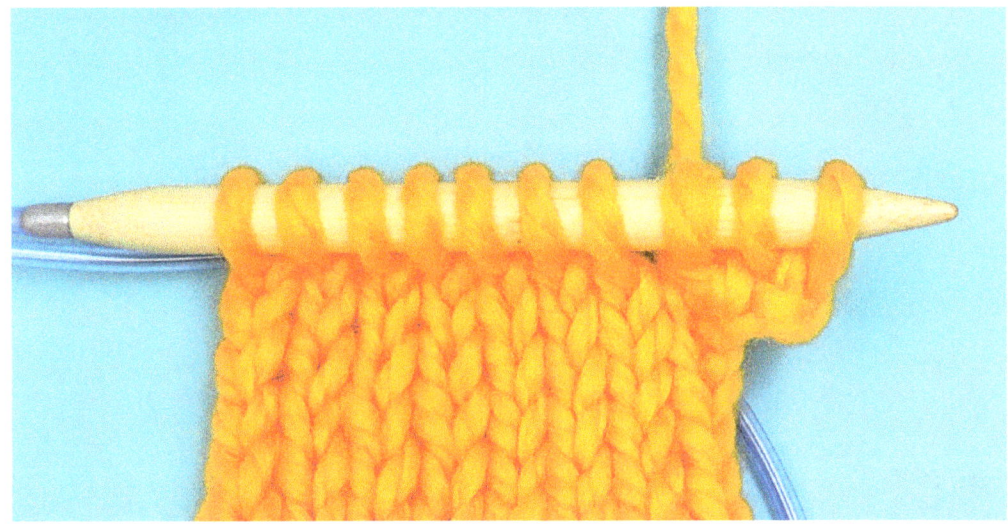

Repeat these steps until the only stitches you have left are the **stitches of the i-cord**. Keep these stitches **on the right needle**.

Now it is time to **join the edges of the i-cord** with an invisible seam. We'll do it by **grafting the live stitches** sitting on the right needle to the corresponding stitches in the very first row of the same i-cord.

STEP 1

Cut the yarn, leaving a **tail that is around 30 cm / 12" long**. Thread this tail into a wool needle. To make it easier for you to see how this method works, I'll use a yarn tail in a contrasting colour.

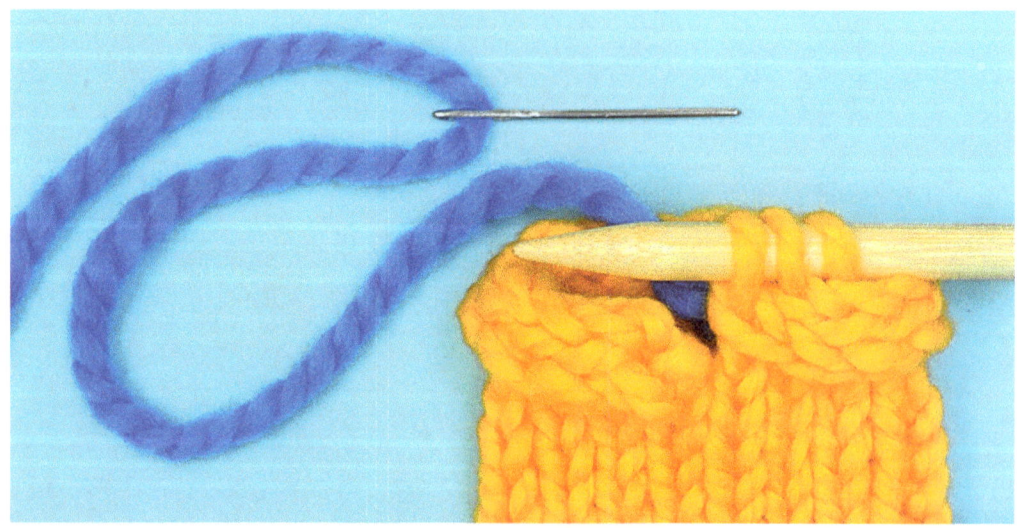

Insert the wool needle **from back to front** into the first stitch from the tip of the knitting needle.

Take this stitch **off the knitting needle** and pull the yarn through. Pull it just enough to keep this stitch **as big as the rest of the live stitches**.

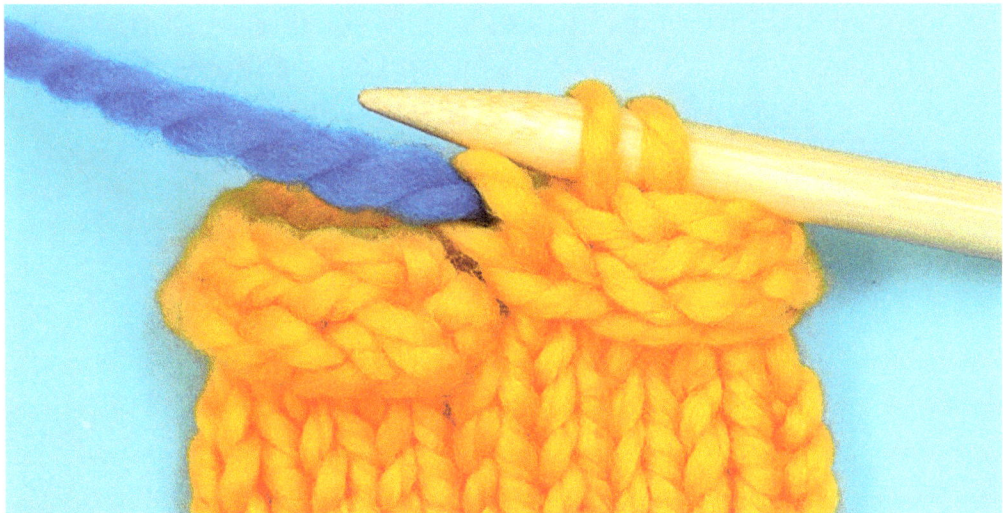

Because this stitch is the first one on the knitting needle, it could be **a bit loose**. If that's the case, pull the yarn some more to **adjust the size of that stitch**, but make sure you **don't tighten it too much**. It should be as big as the rest of the stitches that form the i-cord..

STEP 2

Insert the wool needle **from the bottom up** under both legs of a **corresponding stitch in the first row** of the i-cord.

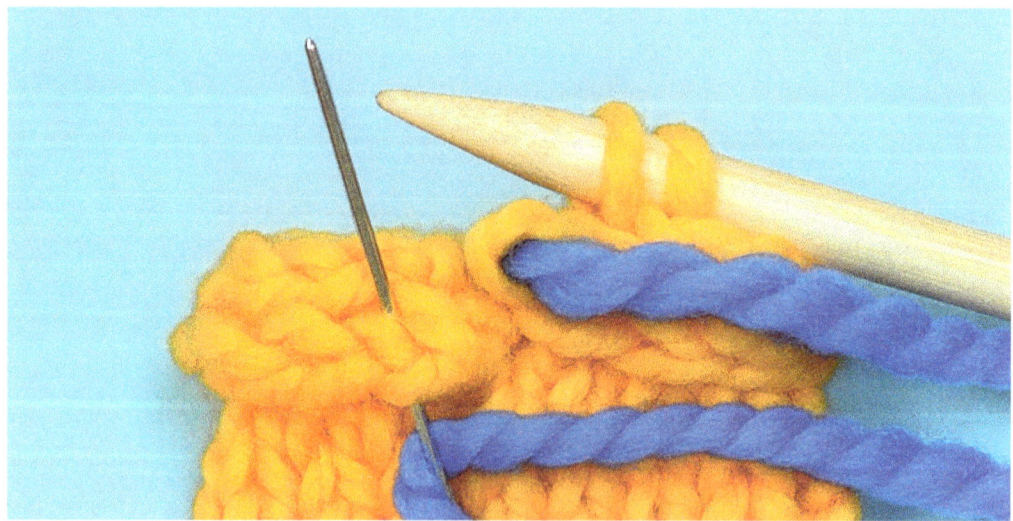

Pull the yarn through so that the strand between the live stitch and the stitch in the first row of the i-cord is **as long as one leg of an average stitch** of this i-cord.

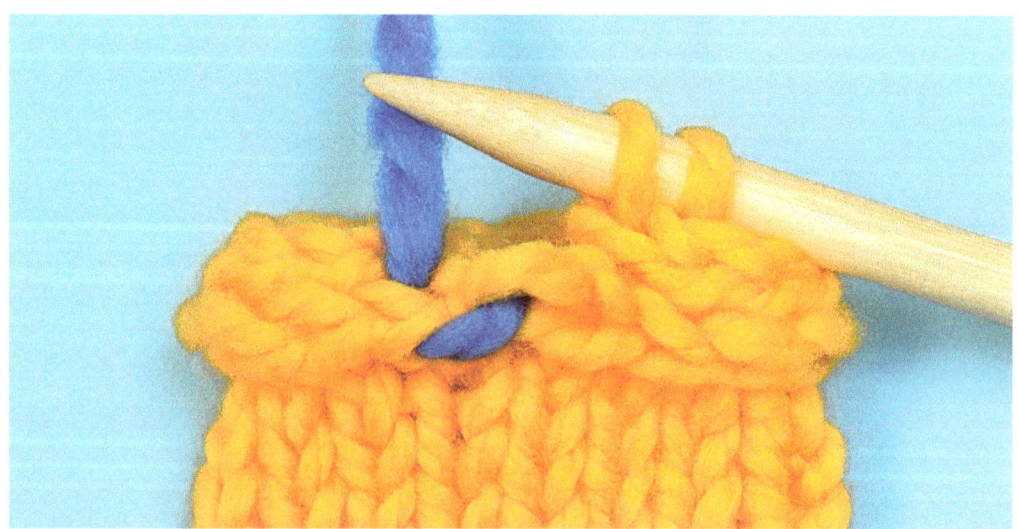

STEP 3

Insert the wool needle **from the top down** into the live stitch that we've just joined to the first row of the i-cord, and **from back to front** into the next stitch on the knitting needle.

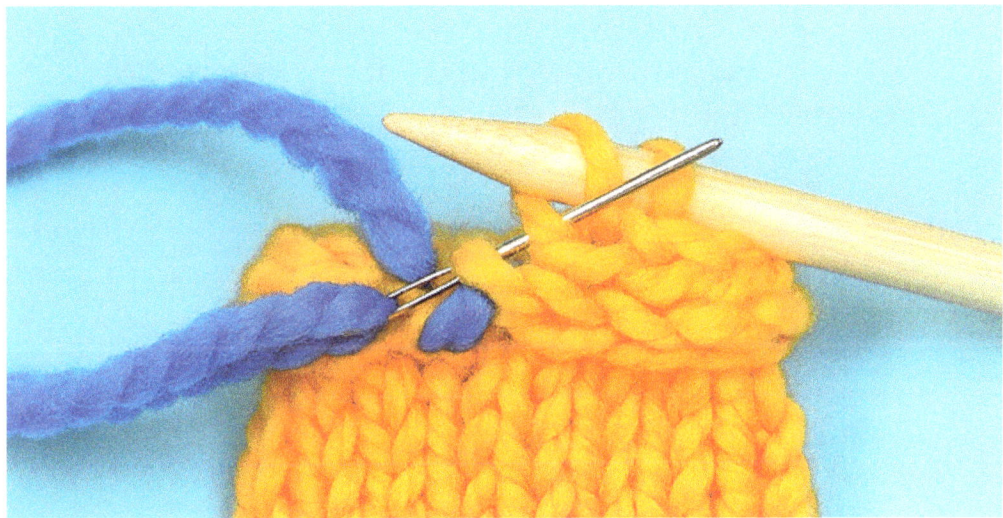

Take this stitch **off the knitting needle** and pull the yarn through both stitches. Don't pull it too tight. The strand between the first row of the i-cord and the live stitches should be **as long as one leg of any stitch** that forms this i-cord.

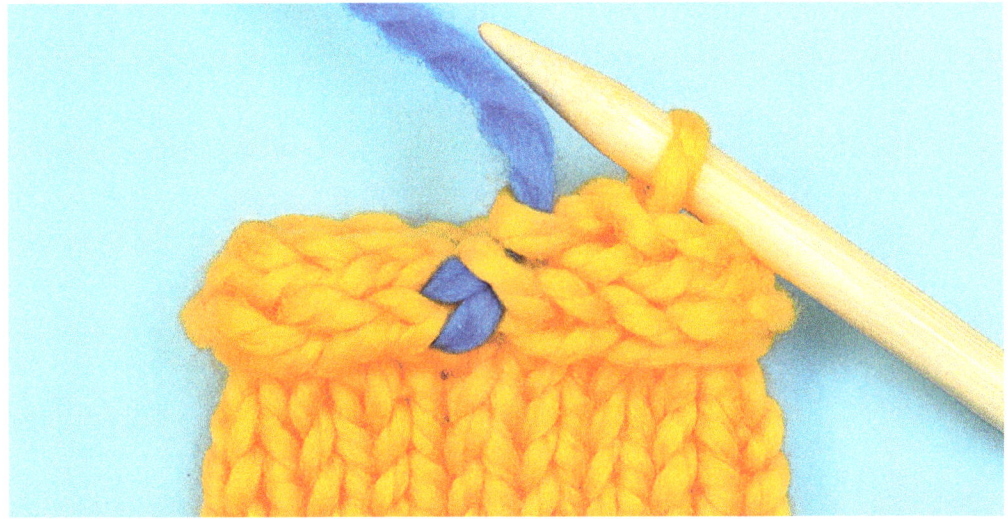

It is very important to **treat this seaming process like embroidery,** being careful when we shape each strand of the seam. This is the key to making this seam fully invisible.

Repeat steps 2 and 3 until you **join all live stitches** to the corresponding stitches in the first row of the i-cord.

Finish by going into the **last stitch of the first row** of the i-cord and pulling the yarn through to **form a "bridge" stitch** between the last live stitch and the first row of the i-cord.

Then insert the wool needle from the top down **into the last live stitch** of the i-cord.

Pull the yarn through and **secure the yarn**. Then **hide the yarn tail** inside the i-cord.

When we use a tail **in the same colour** as the i-cord, the **seam is absolutely invisible**.

As you see, I marked the place of the join with a **stitch marker**. Otherwise, it would be impossible to tell where the seam is.

PURLED I-CORD CAST ON AND PURLED I-CORD BIND OFF

STRETCH ★☆☆☆☆

DIFFICULTY ★★★☆☆

TOOLS

We can easily look at the edges formed by this pair of cast on and bind off methods as **inside-out i-cords**. Because this is exactly what they are—edges treated by an i-cord that proudly **shows off its purl side**.

This unusual look makes these edges a great choice for **projects that need a subtle decoration.** And because these edgings are **fully reversible**, they work well for scarves, blankets, and cardigans as well as other garments and accessories that benefit from lovely edges **with little stretch**.

PURLED I-CORD CAST ON WORKED FLAT

Just as we do when we make an i-cord cast on edge (page 62), we **start by casting on stitches of the i-cord**.

You can go with three to five stitches, but I find that a narrower version looks neater than a wider one, so I'll cast on **three stitches** for an i-cord that will decorate the edge of my swatch.

As for the way of getting those three or more stitches on your needles, **any method will do** as long as it forms a **sturdy edge**—we don't want one side of the cast on edge to flare out.

To start the i-cord on my swatch, I used a **slingshot version of the long-tail cast on** method.

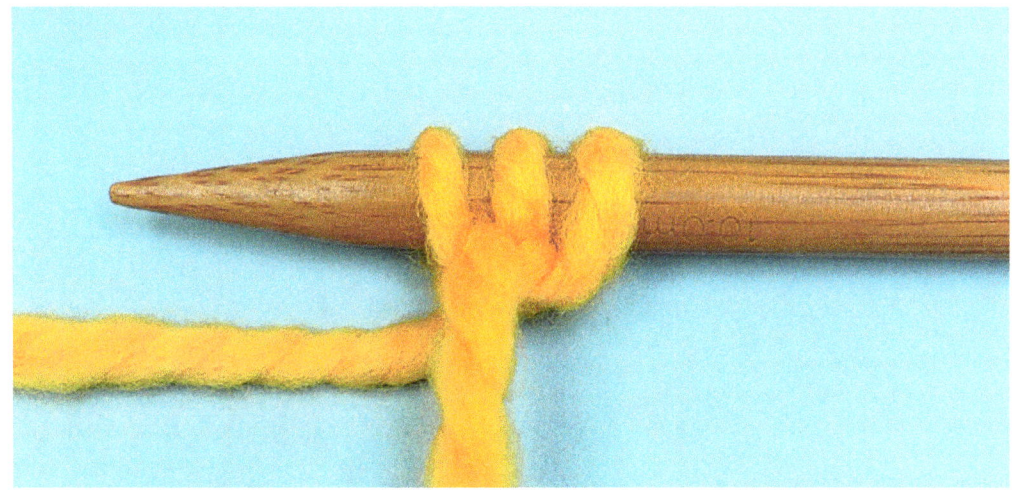

Arrange the work so that the tip of the needle and the working yarn are **on the right-hand side**. That means **turning the work** if you used the long-tail cast on method, **or leaving it as is** if you cast on the stitches of the i-cord using the knitted or cable cast on.

This cast on method boils down to **three simple steps**.

STEP 1

Bring the **yarn to the front** of the work and move it over the right needle to make a **regular yarn over**.

It **might feel a bit awkward** when you form a yarn over **for the first time** because the right needle is not connected to the i-cord yet.

To make it less confusing, simply place the tip of the **right needle under the working yarn and** move the yarn to the back of the needle. The yarn over will be formed on the right needle **without much effort** on your part.

STEP 2

Bring the working **yarn to the front** of the work and purl the stitches of the i-cord.

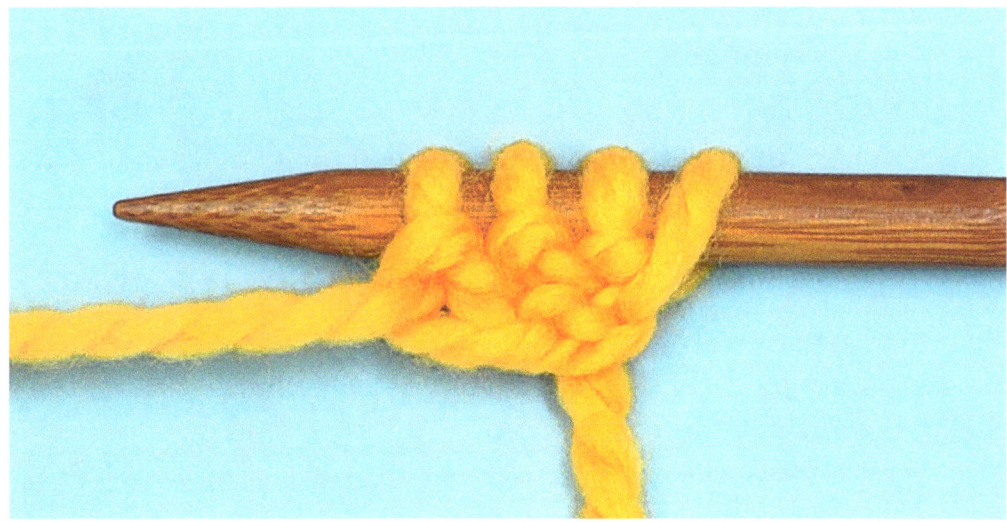

Keep an eye on the yarn over formed in the previous step. Make sure **the yarn goes over the needle** and the yarn over does not disappear after you purl the first stitch.

If that yarn over gets loose, **pull the yarn slightly** after you purl the first stitch to tighten the yarn over.

Usually, the yarn over might get loose **only in the first row** of the i-cord. Once the needles are balanced, the yarn overs behave much better.

STEP 3

Bring the **yarn to the back** of the work and **slip the stitches of the i-cord** to the left needle. Do it **purlwise**, without twisting the stitches.

Repeat these steps **until you cast on** the number of stitches that you need for the project **minus one stitch.** This number **does not include** the stitches of the i-cord. **Finish with step 2** (when the newly-minted stitches and the stitches of the i-cord are still on the right needle).

For example, **to cast on eight stitches** for my swatch, I stop when I have ten stitches on the right needle—**seven cast-on stitches** (eight minus one) **plus three stitches** of the i-cord.

Turn the work.

Purl all stitches of the i-cord together. If the i-cord is made of three stitches, purl those three stitches together. If your i-cord is wider, purl 4 together or purl 5 together depending on the number of stitches you cast on at the very beginning of the cast-on process.

Then bring the **yarn to the back** of the work and **slip the resulting stitch purlwise** to the left needle.

Now we've got **all stitches we need** for the project and we are ready to work the first row.

ROW 1

This is a **wrong-side row** and it can be worked in **two different ways.**

If you add this edge to a **project worked in garter stitch**, or if you want to highlight the edge with a garter ridge on the right side of the fabric, knit all stitches in this row **through the back loop**.

If you add this edge to a project worked in **any other stitch pattern** and you don't want to decorate it with an additional garter ridge, **purl all stitches** in this row **through the back loop**.

Because purling through the back loop is a **slightly tricky** maneuver, I'll break it down into **a few very simple steps**.

With the **yarn at the front** of the work, insert the tip of the right needle **from left to right** under the **back leg** of the first stitch on the left needle.

Wrap the needle with the yarn **as we do when we purl** a stitch.

Pull this yarn wrap through forming a **neat twisted stitch** at the bottom of the right needle, and **slip the worked stitch off** the tip of the left needle.

Once you finish the first row and turn the work, you will see that working each stitch through the back loop produced a lovely **row of twisted stitches** that propped the i-cord, **making it more vivid**.

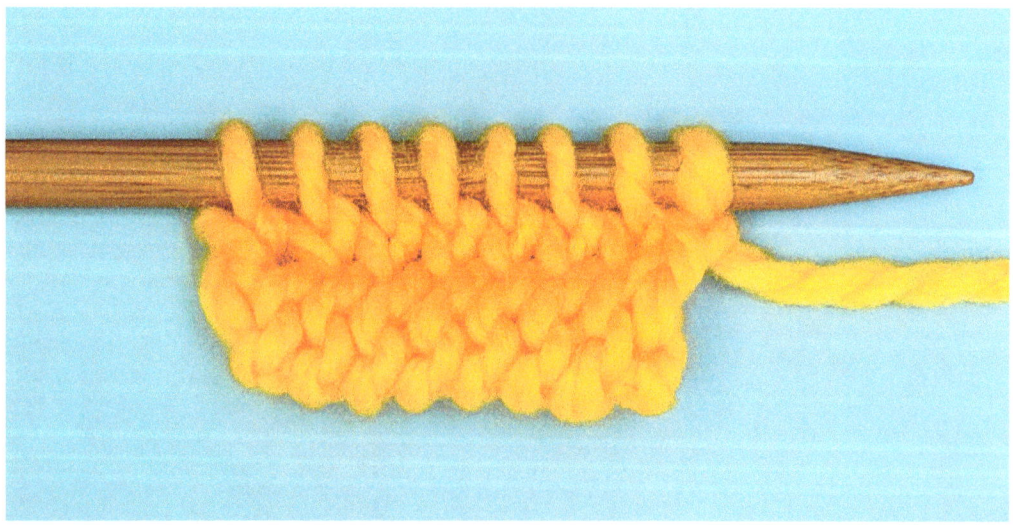

To improve the look of the cast on edge, **pull the i-cord sideways** to redistribute the yarn and **even out the stitches**.

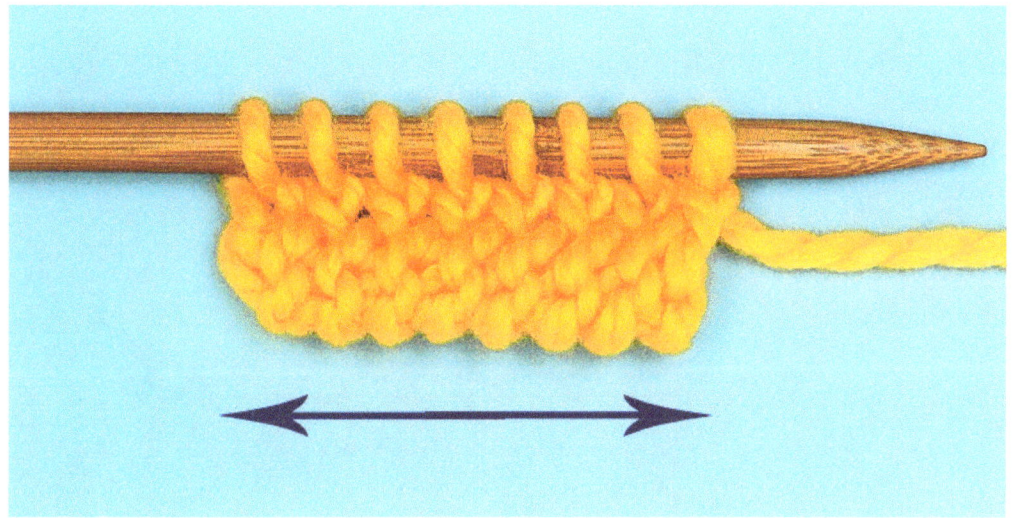

PURLED I-CORD CAST ON WORKED IN THE ROUND

When we want to add this cast on edge to a **seamless project**, we start by casting on **three or more stitches** that will be the foundation of the future i-cord.

Make sure to **leave a pretty long tail** before you cast on the stitches of the i-cord. We'll use this yarn tail **to join the ends of the i-cord** once we cast on all stitches that we need for the project. The yarn tail in my swatch is around 30 cm / 12" long.

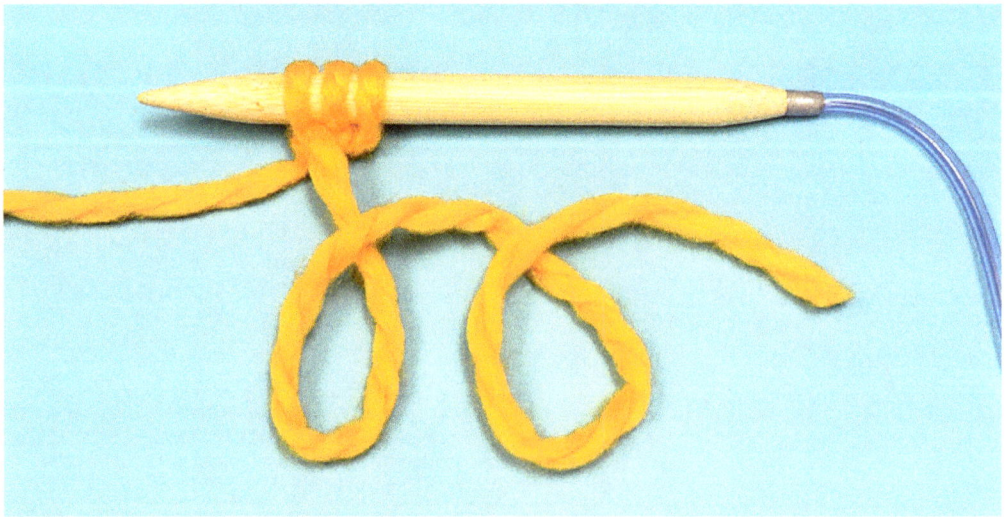

Turn your work if you used the long-tail cast on method or leave it as is if **both the tip of the needle and the working yarn** are already facing **towards the right side**.

Then **follow the same steps** that we performed when we worked **this type of cast on flat**—make a yarn over, purl the stitches of the i-cord and return them back to the left needle while keeping the **yarn at the back** of the work.

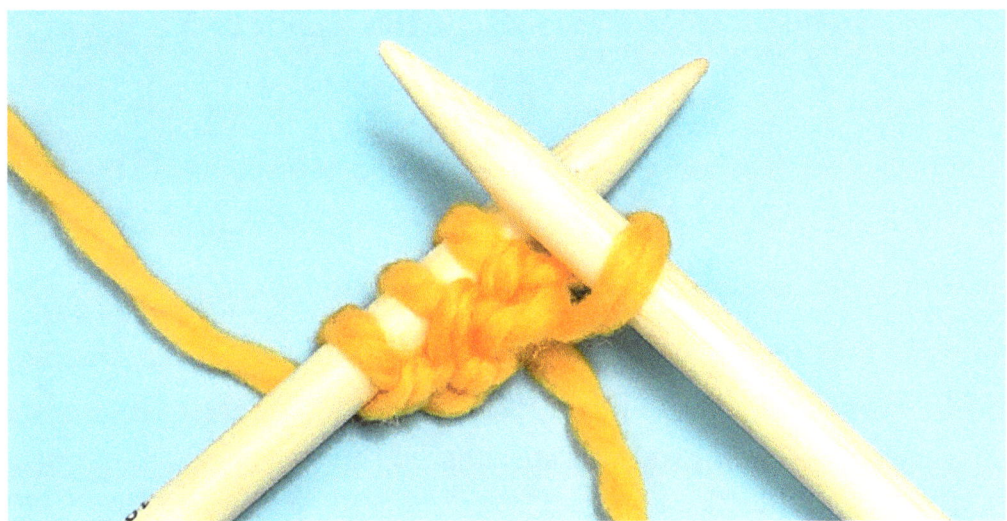

Repeat these steps until you have **all stitches you need for your project** and the stitches of the i-cord sitting on the right needle. **Don't slip** the stitches of the i-cord **to the left needle** after you cast on the last stitch.

To make a swatch on 16 stitches, I stopped when I had 19 stitches on the right needle—16 stitches I need for my swatch plus 3 stitches of the i-cord.

Now it is time for the tricky part—**joining the ends of the i-cord** with a fully invisible seam.

First, arrange the stitches **for working in the round** using any type of setup you like.

I am a big fan of the **magic loop method** so I split the 16 stitches I cast on for the swatch in half and moved the group of 8 stitches to the cord of one circular needle, separating it from the other group of stitches with a loop.

No matter whether you use the magic loop method or a different way to work in the round, **leave the stitches of the i-cord** in the group of stitches that is the **closest to the tip** of the right needle.

As you see, the **first group of stitches** on my needles is made of **8 stitches**, while the group of stitches that is **closer to the tip** of the needle has **11 stitches** in it—8 stitches of the cast on edge plus 3 stitches of the i-cord.

Place the needles so that the first row of the i-cord is **at the left side** and the tip of the needle that holds the stitches of the last row of the i-cord is **on the right**.

Make sure the cast on **edge is not twisted** around the needle. Because the purled i-cord edge is quite thick, you will instantly notice if the edge is twisted. If you do, **fix it right away** because it is much harder to fix a twisted edge once we join the two ends of the i-cord into a circle.

Thread the **long yarn tail** into a wool needle. To help you better see how the process of seaming works, I'll use a yarn tail in a contrasting colour.

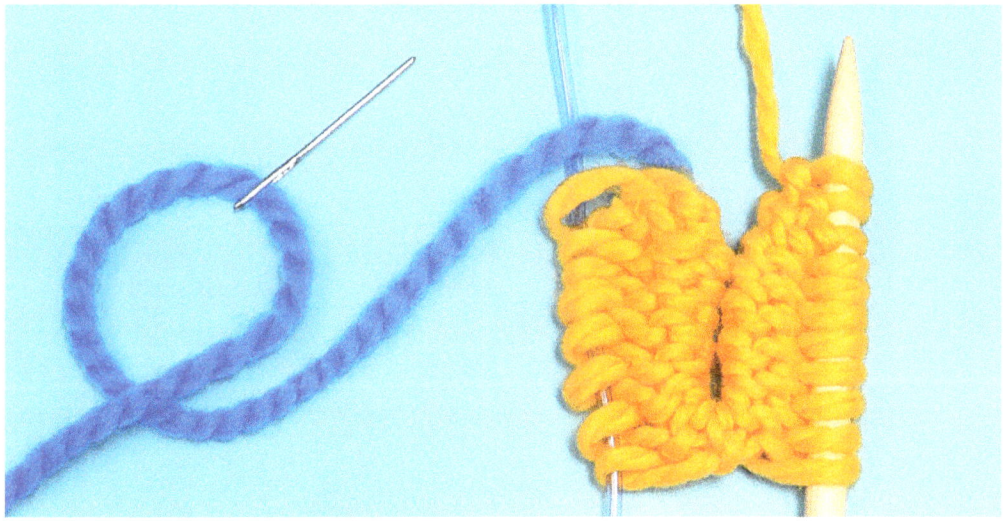

STEP 1

With the working **yarn at the back** of the work, insert the wool needle **from front to back** into the first stitch from the tip of the right needle.

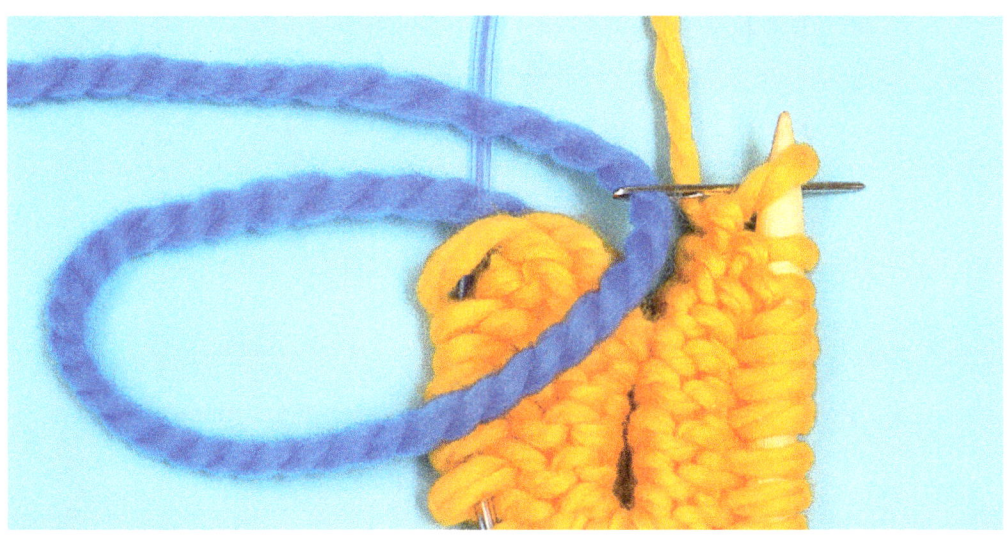

Slip this stitch **off the right needle** and pull the yarn through. Pull it just enough to form a strand that is **as long as one leg of an average stitch** that forms the i-cord.

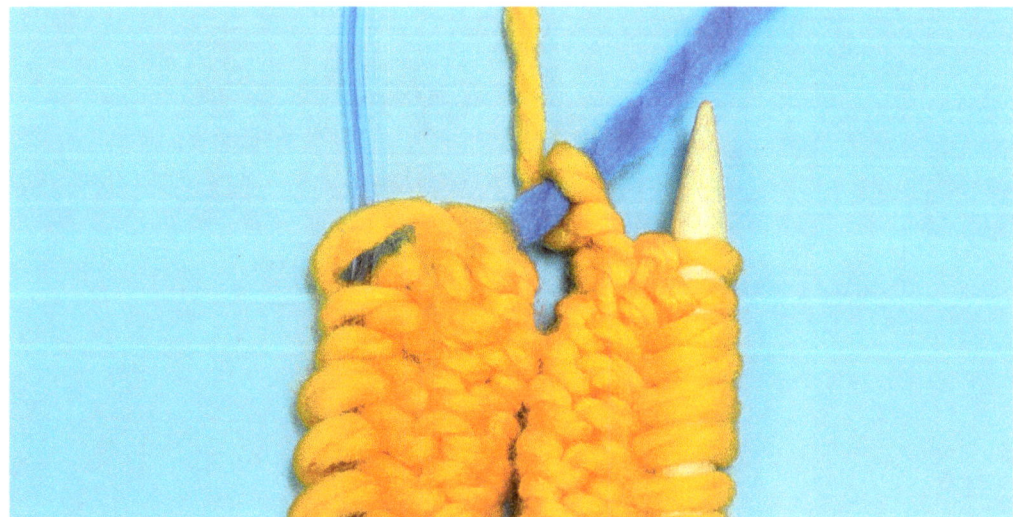

Because this stitch is attached to the working yarn, it can easily become loose. If this happens, **pull the yarn to adjust the size** of the stitch. Be careful not to tighten it too much. It should be as big as the stitches around it.

STEP 2

Now, let's take a look at the **first row of the i-cord** and find the strands that we will join to the live stitches of the i-cord.

The purl side of the fabric tends to be more confusing than the sleek knit side, but this messy look **won't discourage us** because we have a clear guide—the **first loose strand** at the beginning of the i-cord.

This strand is **easy to find**. Simply shift the beginning of the i-cord **a bit to the left** until you see the **loose strands** that join the cast-on stitches with the i-cord.

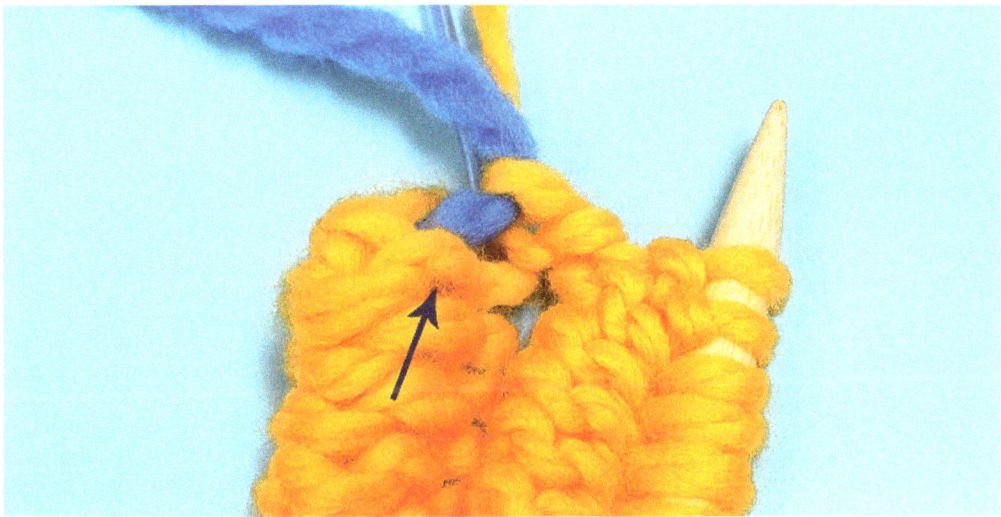

The top strand is the one that we are looking for. It **resembles an arch** or a "frown" nestled next to a "smile". In the photo below, I marked this arch in red.

Look **to the left of this arch** and you will see the arches that correspond to the other stitches of the i-cord. There will be **as many arches as there are stitches** in your i-cord.

Because the i-cord in my swatch is worked over three stitches, I can see **three arches** in the first row of the i-cord.

Insert the wool needle **from the top down** under the **first arch at the right side** of the first row of the i-cord.

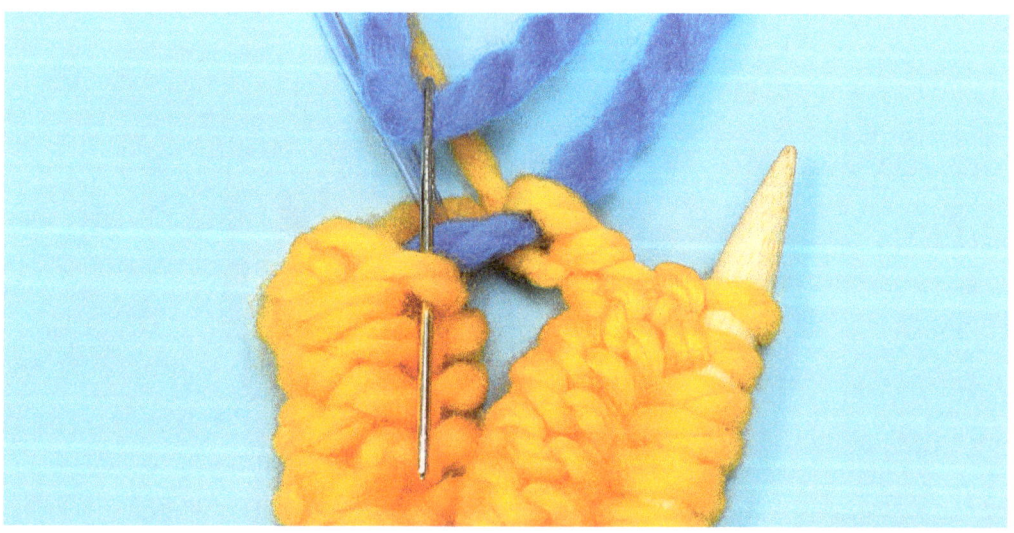

Pull the yarn through and **adjust the size of the strand** to make it as long as one leg of an average stitch of the i-cord.

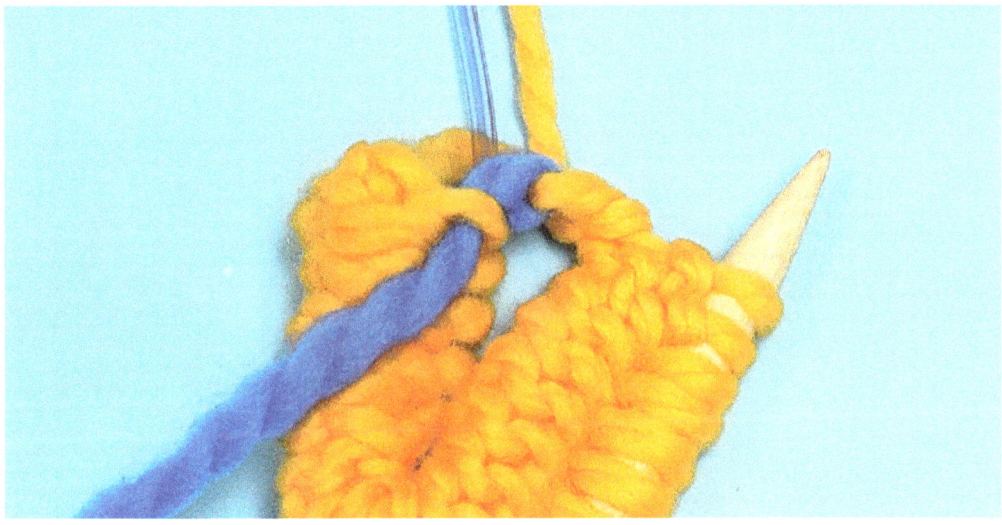

STEP 3

Insert the wool needle **from the bottom up** under the **next arch** and pull the yarn through.

STEP 4

In this step, we go **back to the live stitches** and insert the wool needle **from back to front** into the stitch that we slipped in step 1.

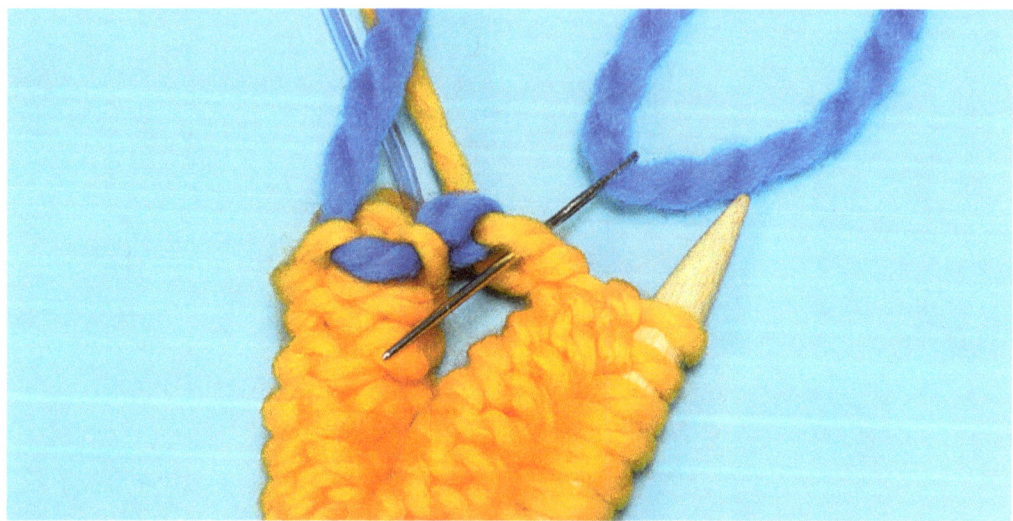

Pull the yarn through and **adjust the size of the strand** to make the seam blend with the stitches of the i-cord.

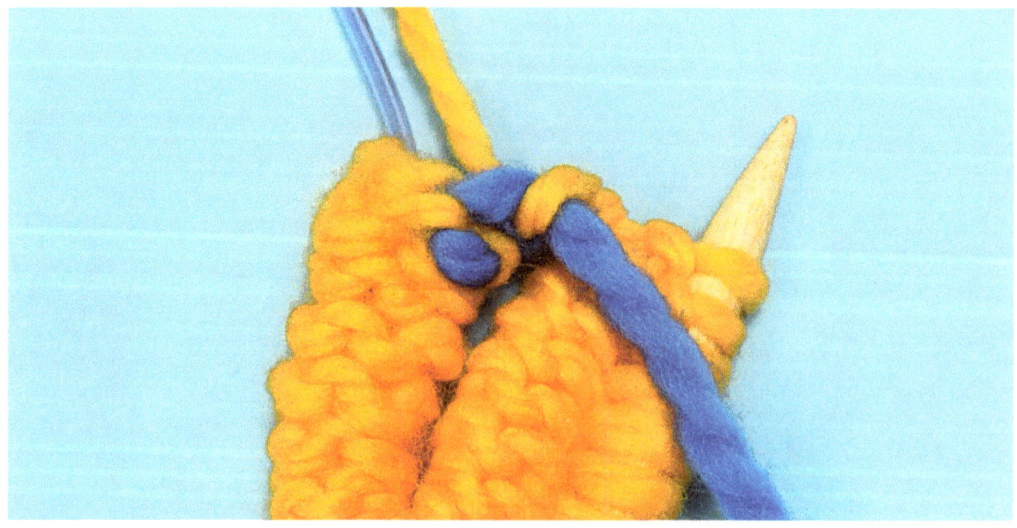

Repeat these four steps until you **join all live stitches to the arches** in the first row of the i-cord.

First, insert the wool needle **from front to back** into the **first stitch** from the tip of the knitting needle. Slip this stitch off the needle and pull the yarn through.

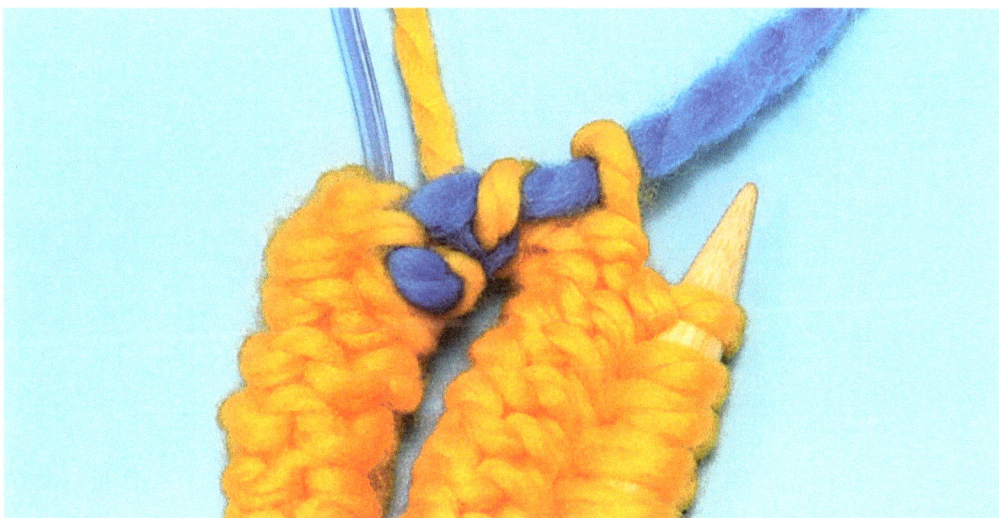

Then insert the wool needle **from the top down** into the arch that we entered three steps ago, and **from the bottom up** into the next arch.

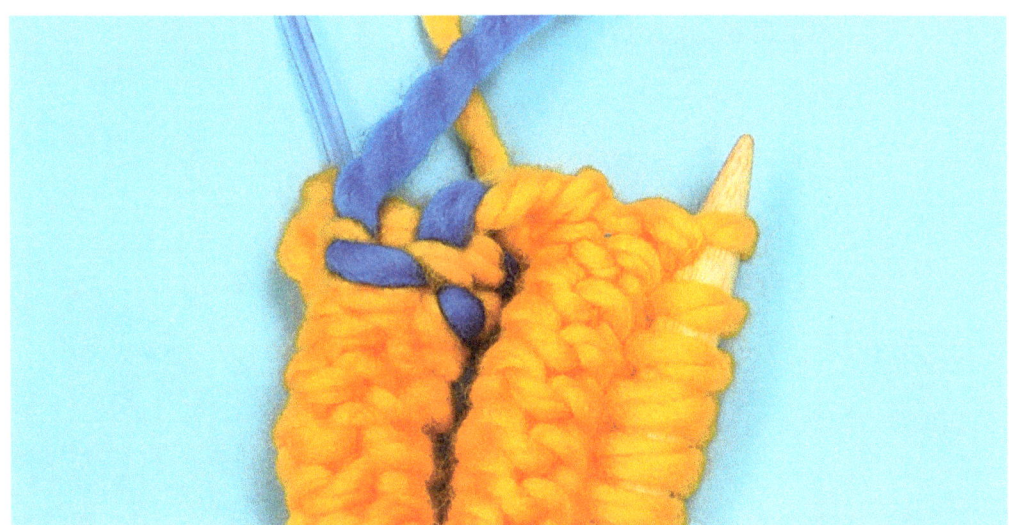

Finally, return to the **recently-slipped stitch** and insert the wool needle into that stitch **from back to front**. Pull the yarn through and adjust the length of the strand.

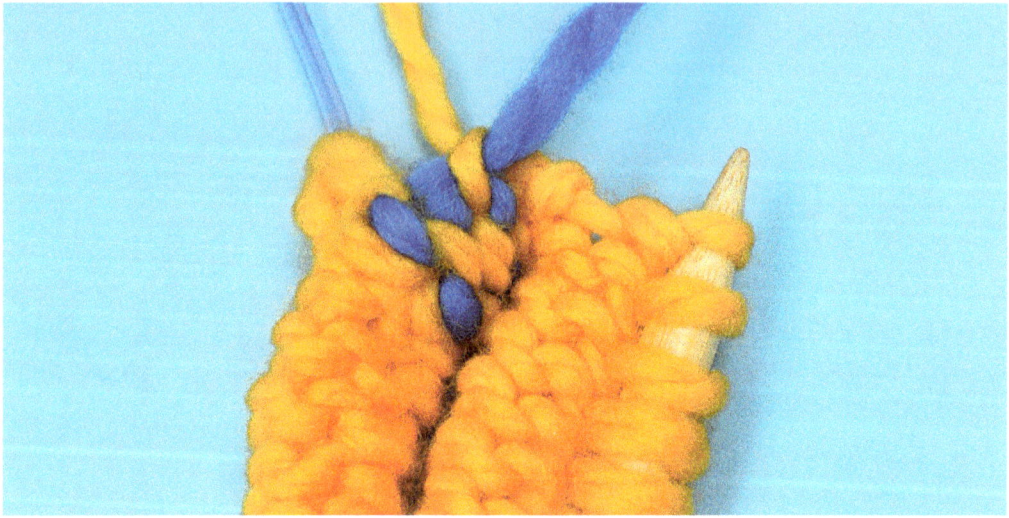

Keep going until you join all live stitches to the corresponding stitches in the first row of the i-cord.

To make the seam **consistent but not too bulky**, don't join the last arch with the first one. Instead, insert the wool needle **from the bottom up** into the nearby stitch.

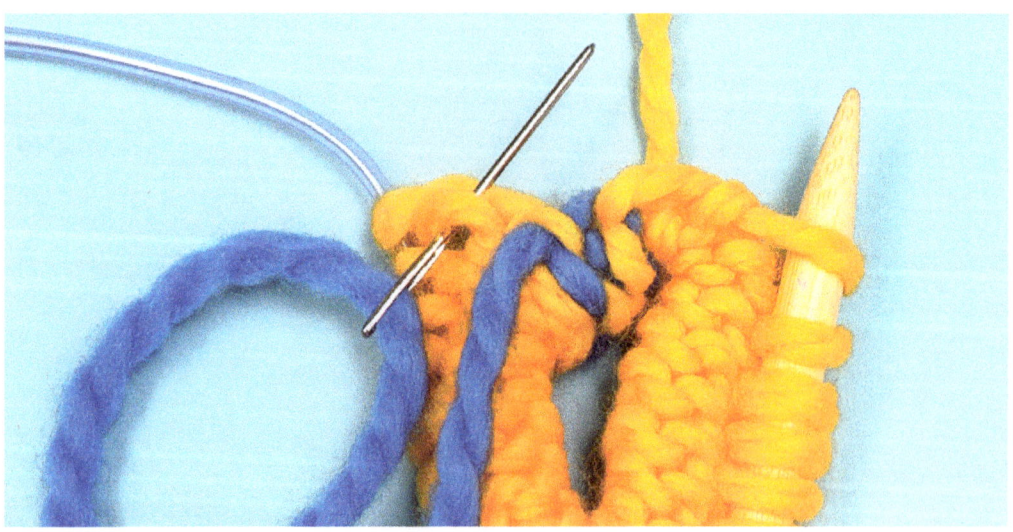

Then go into the **last live stitch** of the i-cord **from back to front**, pull the yarn through, and adjust the size of the strand. If necessary, **redistribute the yarn between stitches** to make the seam as invisible as it can be.

Finally, **secure the yarn** and hide the tail inside the i-cord.

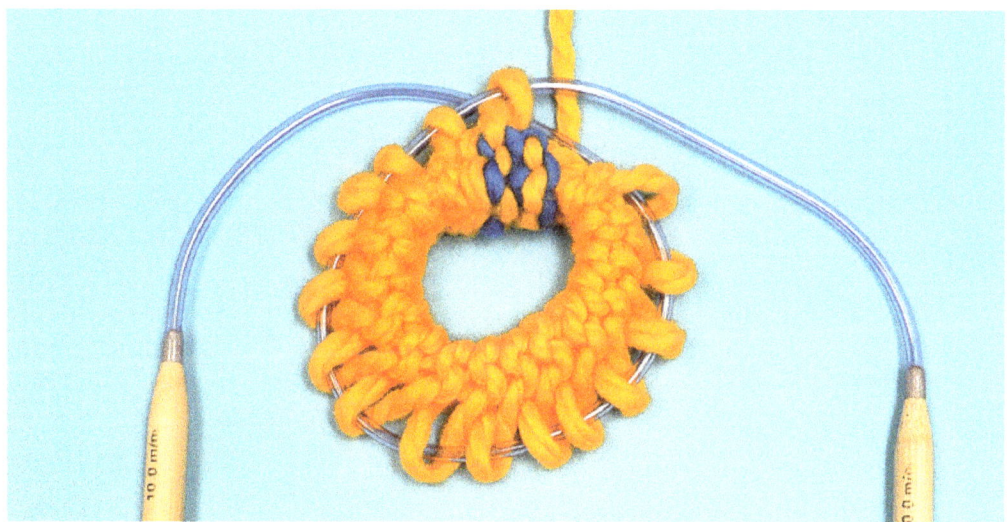

Thanks to the yarn in a contrasting colour, we can clearly see that this seam has **exactly the same structure** as the i-cord. When we make this seam with the **yarn in the same colour** as the project, the seam is **completely invisible**.

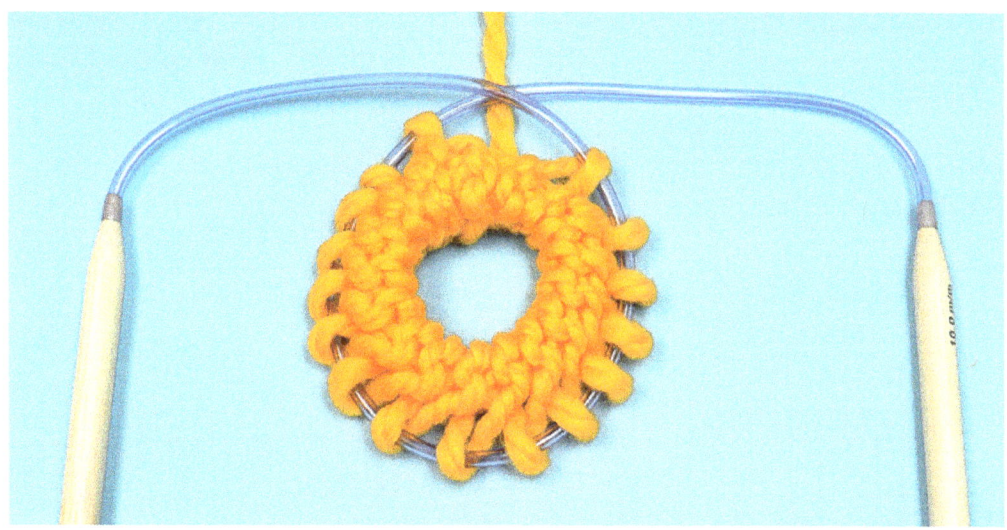

Place a marker that will help you remember where the beginning of the round is, pick up the working yarn, and **work the first round** of your project.

Just as we did when we used this method to cast on stitches for a project worked flat, we'll work the stitches of the first round **through the back loop**.

Knitting and purling through the back loop will form a **set of twisted stitches** that will look neat and will **prop the i-cord edge** to help it shine as a subtle decoration to your project.

If the **first cast-on stitch** was bigger than the rest of the stitches, it might form a hole at the place of joining. To fix this, **stretch the i-cord** and redistribute the yarn between the stitches of the first round.

If this doesn't close the hole completely, seal the hole with a **couple of overhand stitches**. It is an easy fix that works every time.

PURLED I-CORD BIND OFF WORKED FLAT

Now that we know how to add an inside-out i-cord to the cast on edge of our project, let's see how we can make an **identical edge when we bind off** stitches.

To match the **look of the twisted stitches** in the first row of the project, work the stitches of the last wrong-side row **through the back loop**. If you work in stockinette stitch, purl all stitches through the back loop as described on page 101.

If your project is made in a different stitch pattern, work the stitches the same way as you did **right after you cast on stitches** using the purled i-cord cast on method.

Turn your work so that the **right side of the fabric is facing you**.

Just as we do any time we want to add an i-cord to a horizontal edge, we **start by casting on stitches** that will be the foundation of that i-cord.

Depending on the width of the i-cord you plan to make, cast on **three to five stitches**. If you are after a **prominent thick edge**, cast on four or five stitches, but if you want to make the edge look **sleeker and neater**, cast on three stitches.

It is also important to consider the **width of the i-cord at the cast on edge** if you want the bind off edge to match that look.

The bottom of my swatch is decorated with a purled i-cord worked on **three stitches**, so this is the number of stitches that I am going to cast on before I start to bind off stitches.

I do this by using the **knitted cast on** method—the same way we used when we started the i-cord bind off described on page 80.

STEP 1

Bring the **yarn to the front** of the work and purl all stitches **to the last stitch of the i-cord**. For my swatch, this means purling two stitches.

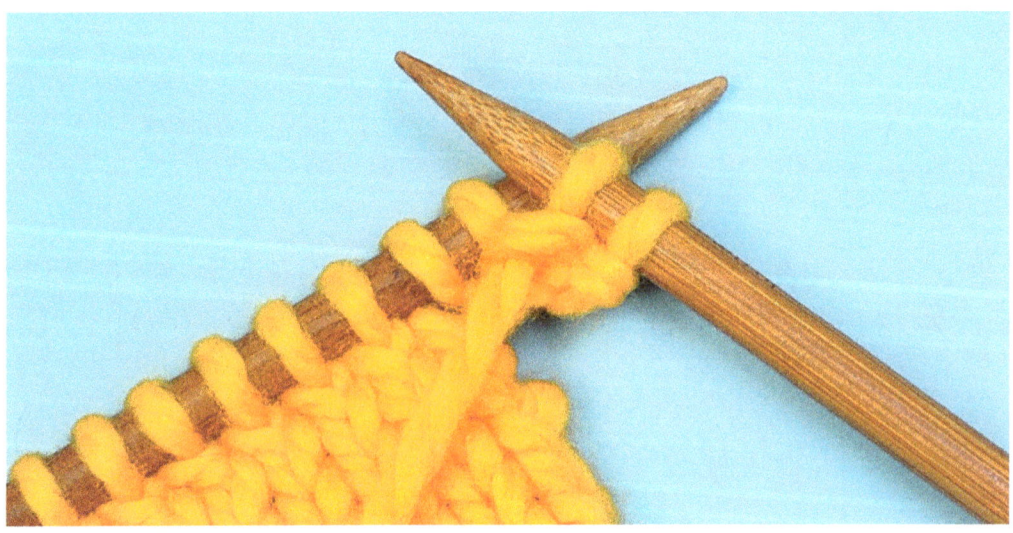

STEP 2

With the **yarn still in front** of the work, insert the tip of the right needle **from right to left** into the last stitch of the i-cord and into the next stitch sitting on the left needle.

Wrap the tip of the right needle with the yarn **as we do when we purl** a stitch and pull this wrap through, purling these **two stitches together**. Slip the purled stitches off the left needle.

We've just worked one row of the i-cord and **bound off one stitch**.

STEP 3

Now bring the **yarn to the back** of the work and **slip the resulting stitches** one by one from the right needle to the left needle. To avoid twisting these stitches, insert the tip of the left needle into each stitch **from left to right**.

Repeat these three steps until you bind off all stitches of the main fabric and there are only the stitches of the i-cord left on your right needle. There is **no need to slip the remaining stitches** to the left needle after you bind off the last stitch.

To finish off the work, cut the yarn leaving a small tail. Thread that tail into a wool needle and slip the remaining stitches from the knitting needle **to the wool needle**.

Pull the yarn to **tighten the stitches** and secure the yarn. Then **weave in the tail**, hide it inside the i-cord, and enjoy the lovely bind off edge that you've just formed.

PURLED I-CORD BIND OFF WORKED IN THE ROUND

Things get **a little bit more complicated** when we use this bind off method to close stitches of a **seamless project**.

To match the look of the twisted stitches in the first round of the project, we **work the last round** by knitting or purling all stitches **through the back loop**.

As my swatch is worked in stockinette stitch, in the last round I knitted each stitch through the back loop.

We start the bind-off round by **casting on three to five stitches** for the future i-cord, and we do it using the **knitted cast on** (page 80) or a similar method.

122 | MATCHING CAST ONS & BIND OFFS

Then we **repeat the same three steps** that we followed when we added this edging to a **project worked flat**. We stop when we **bind off all stitches** of the main fabric, and we are left only with the stitches of the i-cord. In my case, it is three stitches.

Leave the remaining stitches **on the right needle**.

Cut the yarn, leaving a yarn tail that is around 30 cm / 12" long and **thread this tail into a wool needle**. To make each step of the process easier to see, I will use a yarn tail in a contrasting colour.

Now comes the most interesting part of the process—**joining the live stitches** of the i-cord to the ones we cast on **at the very beginning** of the bind-off round.

Remember the **"arches"** we were looking for when we joined the purled i-cord in the round at the cast on edge (page 109)? We will need to **find these strands** in the first row of the i-cord to make sure the seam is **completely invisible**.

These strands are at the **right-hand side of the first purl ridge** at the very beginning of the i-cord, and there are as many of them as there are stitches in the i-cord. In my swatch, there are three.

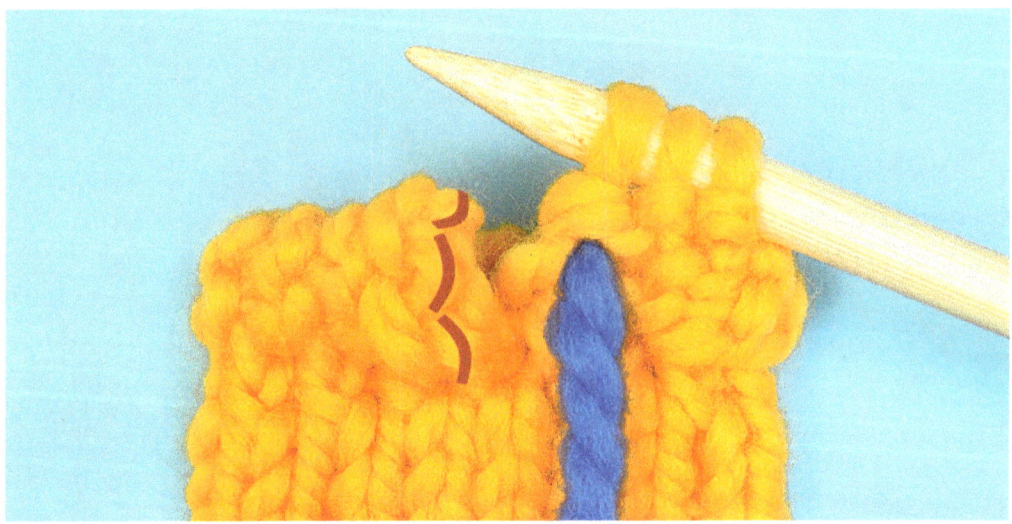

Once we find those strands, we are ready to **join them to the live stitches** still sitting on the right needle.

STEP 1

Insert the wool needle **from front to back** into the first stitch from the tip of the right needle.

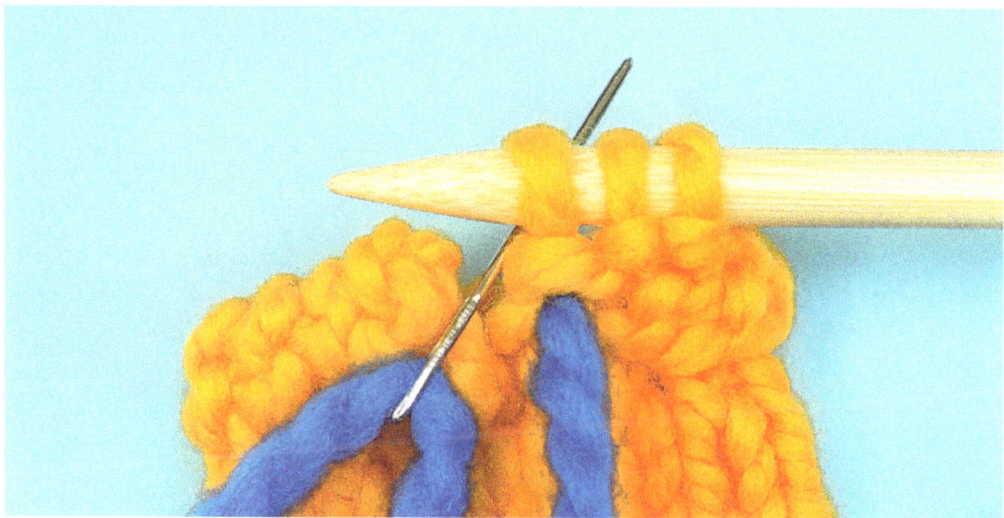

Slip this stitch **off the needle** and pull the yarn through.

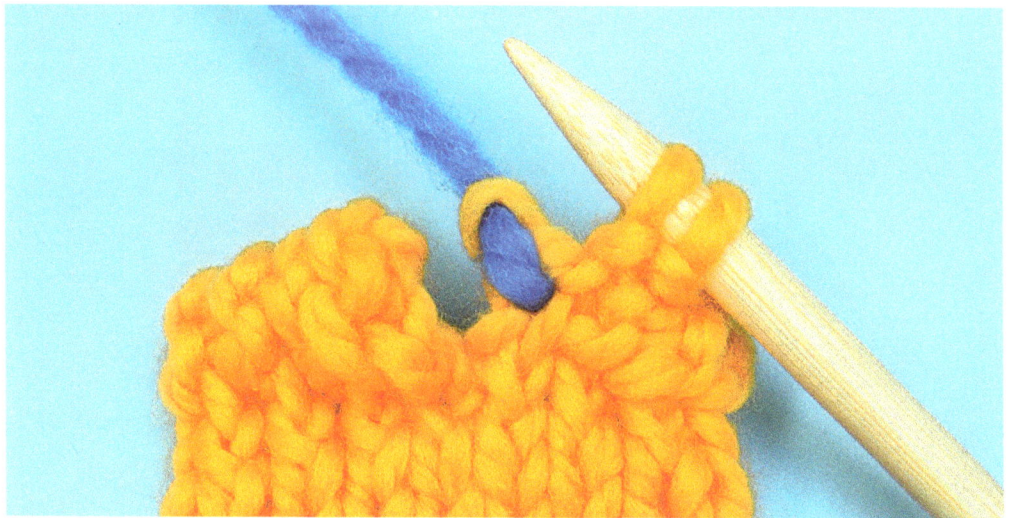

If necessary, **pull the yarn some more** to make this stitch as big as the rest of the stitches of the i-cord.

STEP 2

Insert the wool needle **from right to left** under the arch that corresponds to the slipped stitch.

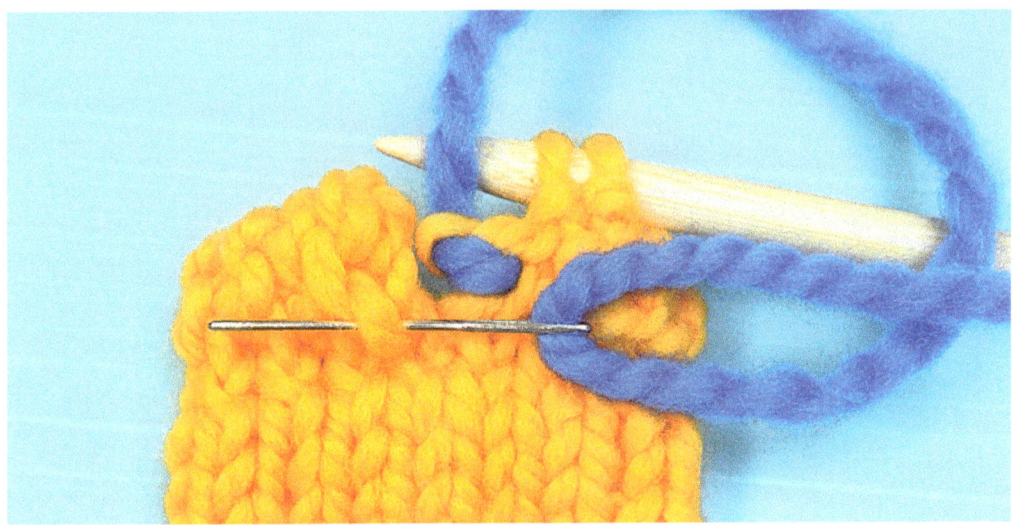

Pull the yarn through, making sure the strand between the slipped stitch and the arch is **as long as one leg of an average stitch** of the i-cord.

STEP 3

Insert the wool needle **from left to right** under the next arch and pull the yarn through.

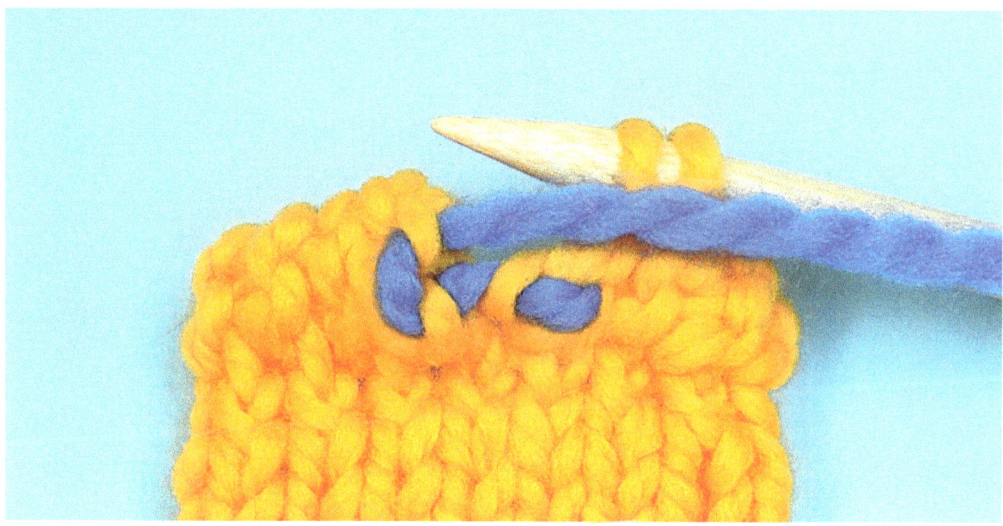

STEP 4

Go back to the **slipped stitch** and insert the wool needle into that stitch **from back to front**.

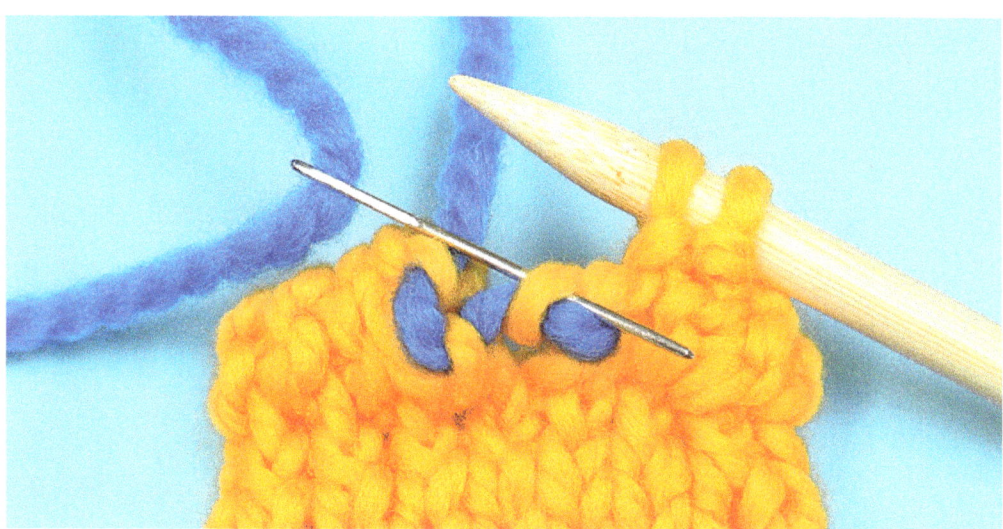

Repeat these four steps until you join all live stitches to the corresponding strands in the first row of the i-cord. Stop when the yarn is coming out **at the left side of the last arch**.

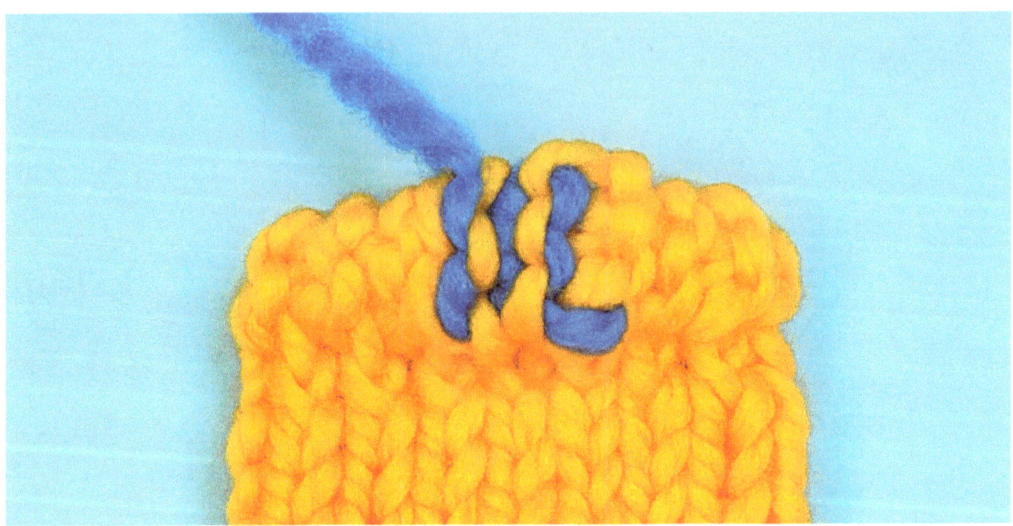

LAST STEP

Insert the wool needle **from left to right** under the "bump" at the back of the stitch that we joined to the first live stitch and **from back to front** into the last live stitch.

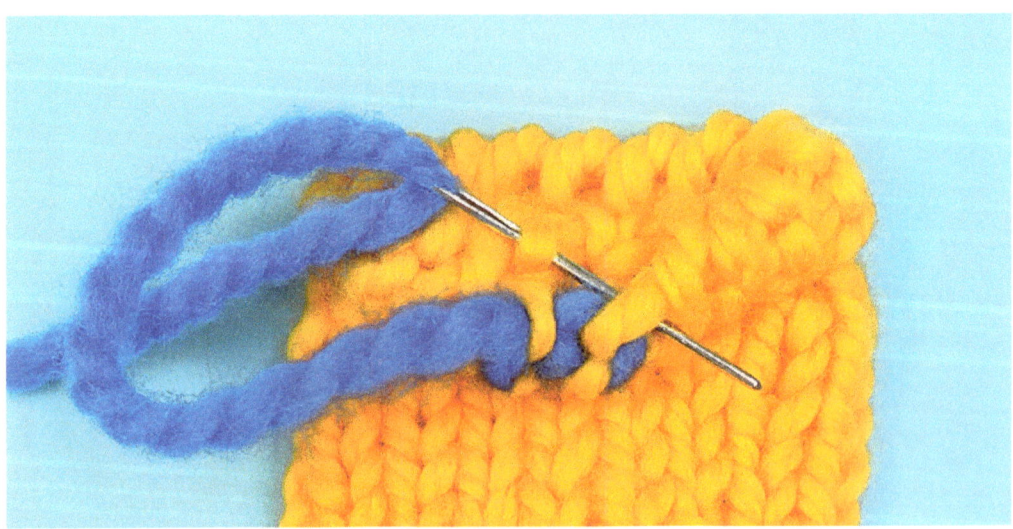

Pull the yarn through and **adjust the length of the strand**.

Secure the yarn and **hide the yarn tail** inside the i-cord.

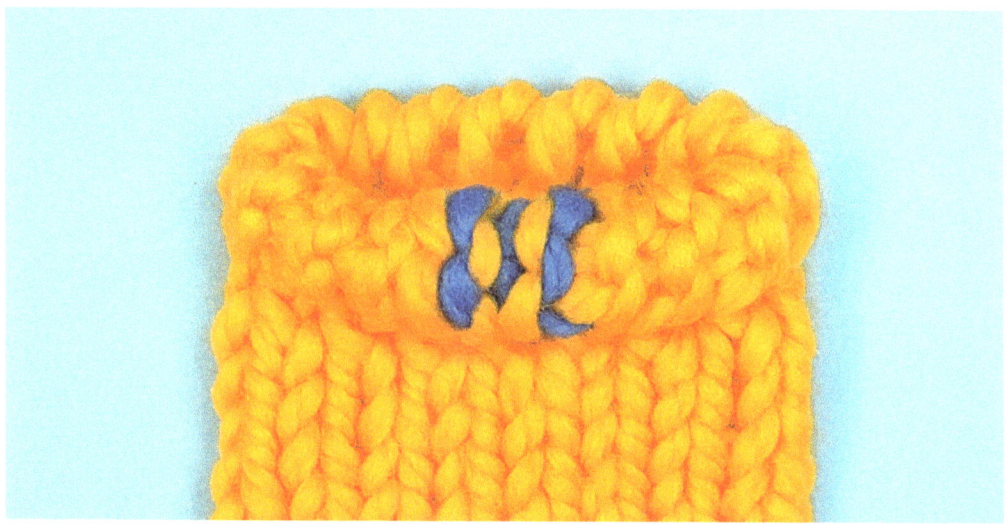

Because we were careful to **join each live stitch to a corresponding strand** in the first row of the i-cord, the seam we formed is **fully invisible**.

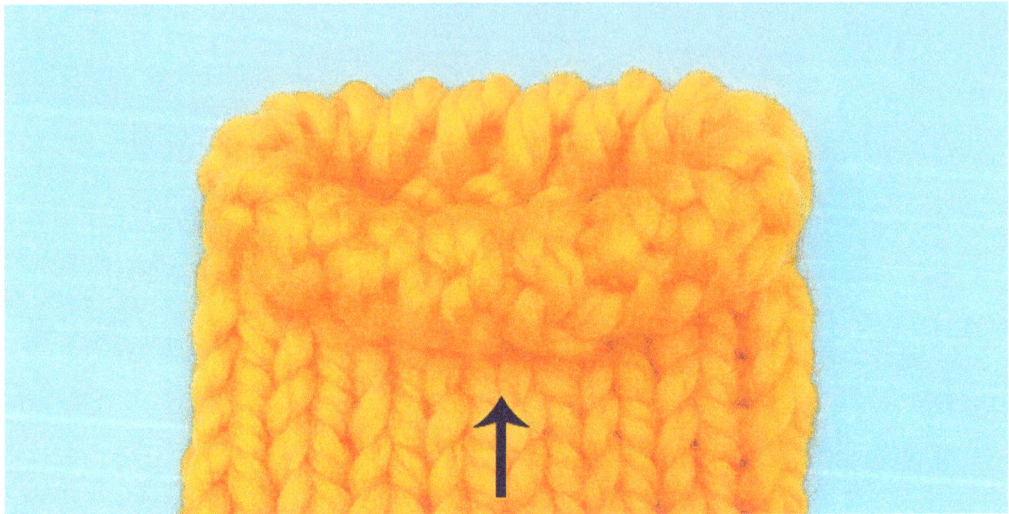

When the stitches are joined using the **yarn tail in the same colour** as the project, no one will be able to tell where the seam is.

BRAIDED CAST ON AND BRAIDED BIND OFF

STRETCH ★☆☆☆☆

DIFFICULTY ★★☆☆☆

TOOLS

We'll finish this section of the book by taking a look at a pair of methods that are **based on i-cord** but form edges that look **more like braids** than cords.

This happens because we **reduce the width of the i-cord** to two stitches, and this little tweak completely changes the outcome.

Instead of an i-cord, we see a set of braids that decorate **every facet of the edge**—one braid at the front, one at the back, and one at the very bottom of the edge.

This structure makes these edges **fully reversible and very neat**. They look great on scarves, blankets, sweaters, cardigans, and all other projects that do not require highly elastic edges.

BRAIDED CAST ON WORKED FLAT

We start by **casting on two stitches** that will form the braid at the cast on edge. Do it by using the **knitted cast on** (page 80), cable cast on, or any other cast on method that forms a **sturdy cast on edge**.

To get those initial stitches on my needles, I used a **slingshot version of the long-tail cast on** method.

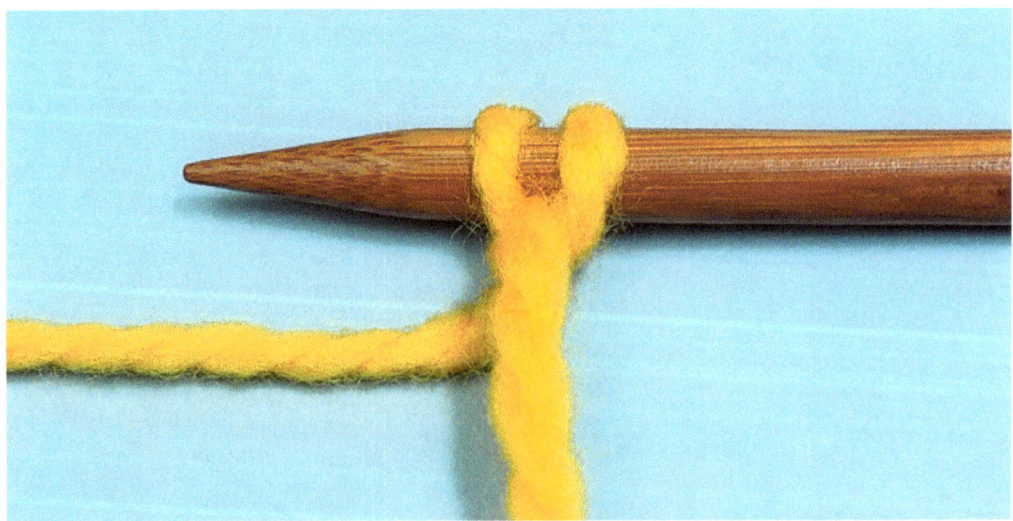

Arrange the work so that the tip of the needle is **pointing to the right** and the working yarn is **at the right side** of the newly-minted stitches.

Take the needle with the stitches in your left hand, and an empty needle in your right hand.

STEP 1

Move the working **yarn to the back** of the work, and bring it over the right needle to form a **reverse yarn over**.

This step could feel a bit awkward when we do it **for the first time** because the right needle is **not connected to the work yet** and the needles are not balanced.

To make it easier, place the right needle **on the working yarn** and move the yarn over the top of the needle and to its front.

STEP 2

Bring the **yarn to the back** of the work and knit both stitches sitting on the left needle.

Keep an eye on the **yarn over**. Make sure you **don't lose it** after you knit the first stitch of the braid.

STEP 3

Slip two stitches from the right needle to the left needle.

To avoid twisting these stitches, insert the tip of the left needle into each stitch **from left to right**, and then move the right needle out of that stitch leaving it on the left needle.

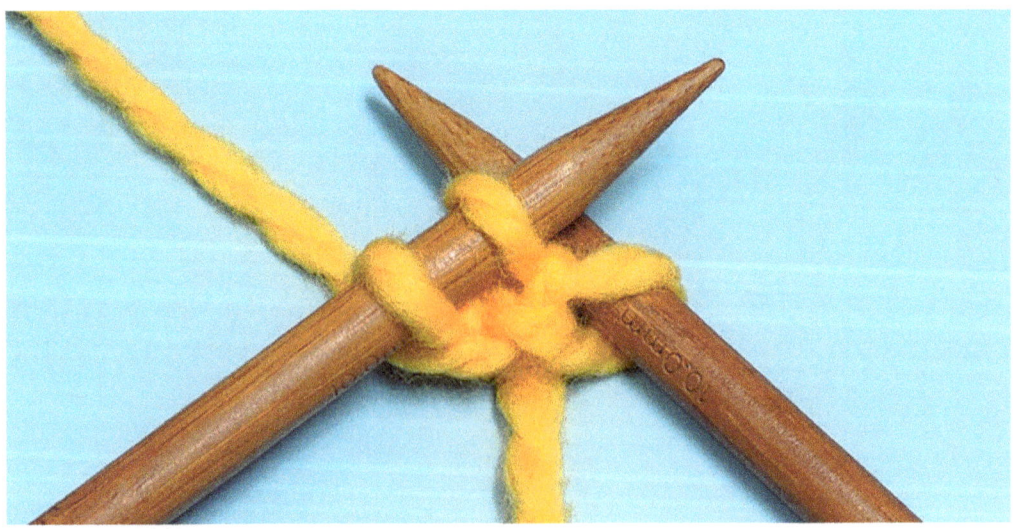

Repeat these three steps until the right needle holds the number of stitches that you need for your project **minus one stitch**, and two stitches of the braid are on the left needle.

For example, to cast on 8 stitches for my swatch I stop when I have 7 stitches on my right needle and 2 stitches on my left needle.

LAST STEP

With the working **yarn at the back** of the work, insert the tip of the right needle **from right to left** into the second stitch on the left needle.

Pass this stitch **over the first stitch** and off the left needle.

Slip the remaining stitch to the right needle. Do it **purlwise**, without twisting the stitch.

Now the number of stitches on the right needle is the **number we need for the project**, so we can turn the needle and **work the first row** as instructed in the pattern.

To show you how this cast on edge looks **next to a textured pattern**, I worked my swatch in seed stitch (known as "moss stitch" in the UK).

To make sure **none of the stitches forms a hole** in the first row of the project, knit or purl each stitch as usual **through the front loop**.

If the pattern instructions include **twisted stitches** worked through the back loop, **replace those stitches** with regular knits and purls as you work **the first row**.

BRAIDED CAST ON WORKED IN THE ROUND

Out of all cast on methods based on i-cord, the braided cast on is **the easiest one** to add to a seamless project. The braid has **only two stitches**, and joining them to the corresponding live stitches is much easier than joining stitches of a wider i-cord.

But before we get to join the stitches, we have quite a few stitches to cast on, and we start by making **two stitches that will be the foundation** of the future three-faceted braid.

Before you cast on these stitches, make sure you **leave a longer tail**. To be on the safe side, I usually leave a tail that is around 30 cm / 12" long.

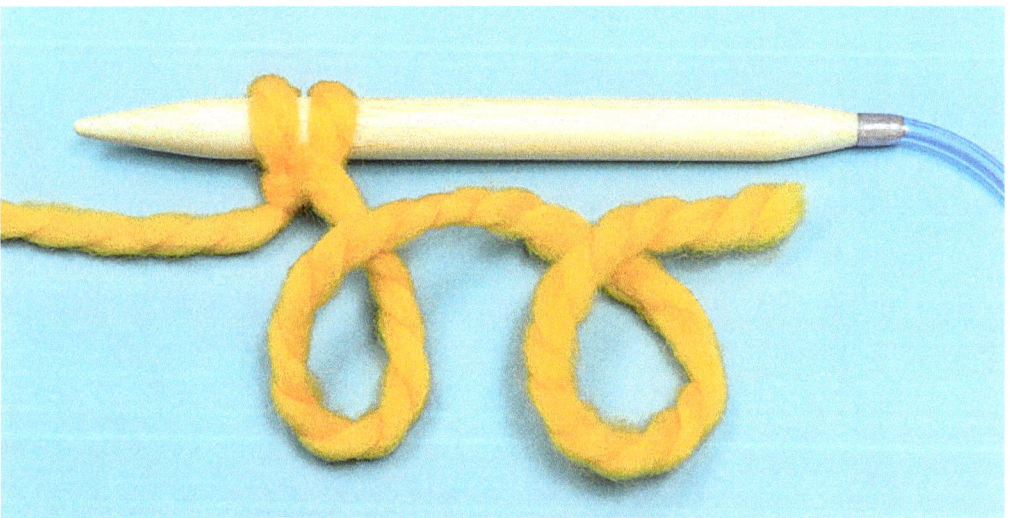

Arrange the work so that both the working yarn and the tip of the needle are **at the right-hand side** of the stitches, and **repeat the same three steps** that we followed when we used this method to cast on stitches for a project worked flat—make a reverse yarn over, knit two stitches, then slip those two stitches purlwise to the left needle.

Repeat these steps until you have the number of stitches that you need for your project **plus two stitches of the braid** nestled on your **right needle**.

For example, to cast on 16 stitches for my swatch, I stop when I have 18 stitches on my right needle, while the left needle is empty.

Even though we cast on stitches for a seamless project, we don't work in the round just yet. We'll be ready for that part right after we **join the two stitches that we cast on** at the very beginning of the cast-on process **to the two live stitches** that are now the first and the second stitches from the tip of the right needle.

First, **let's arrange the work** so that we can clearly see the stitches we are about to join.

To do this, you can divide all stitches between four or five **double-pointed needles**, divide them between **two short circular needles**, spread them along the length of **one circular needle**, or split them in half on one long circular needle if you plan to use the **magic loop method** as I do.

No matter what setup you use to work in the round, keep **two stitches of the braid** in the group of stitches that is the **closest to the tip** of the right needle.

Thread the **yarn tail** that was formed at the cast on edge **into a wool needle**. To make it easier for you to see what is happening on my needles, I'll use a yarn tail in a contrasting colour.

Make sure the cast on **edge is not twisted**. It is very easy to notice a twisted edge with a thicker cast on edge like the one formed by the braided cast on method, but still it is worth taking a moment to **double check** that the edge is nice and even.

A twisted cast on edge is one of the few knitting mistakes that **cannot be fixed without undoing the work**, so it is better to be alert every time we join stitches for working in the round.

STEP 1

With the working **yarn at the back** of the work and out of the way, insert the wool needle **from back to front** into the first stitch from the tip of the right needle.

Slip this stitch off the knitting needle and pull the yarn through, but **don't pull it too much**. The strand between the two sides of the braid should be **as long as one leg of an average stitch** that forms the braid.

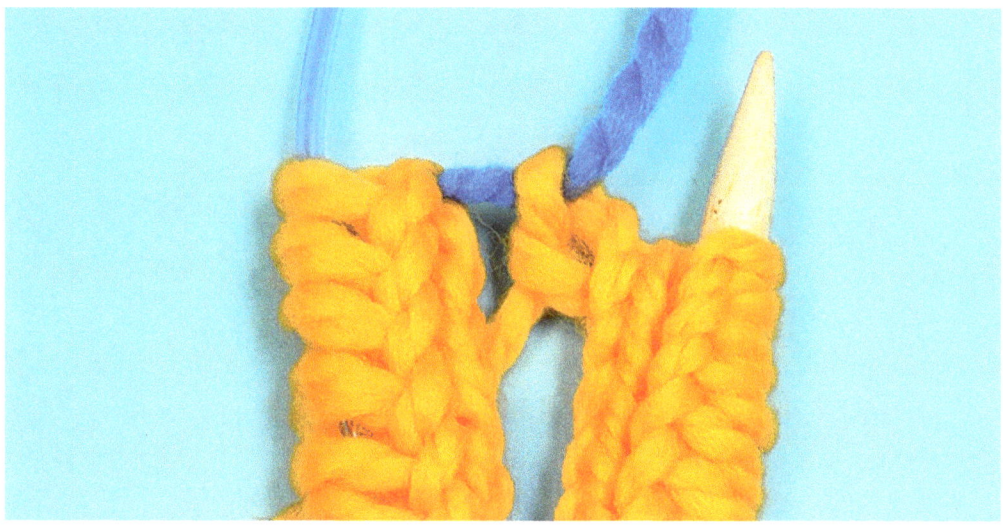

STEP 2

Insert the wool needle **from right to left** under both legs of the first stitch at the right side of the first row of the braid. Because the **braid is now upside down**, this stitch looks like an **inverted "V"**.

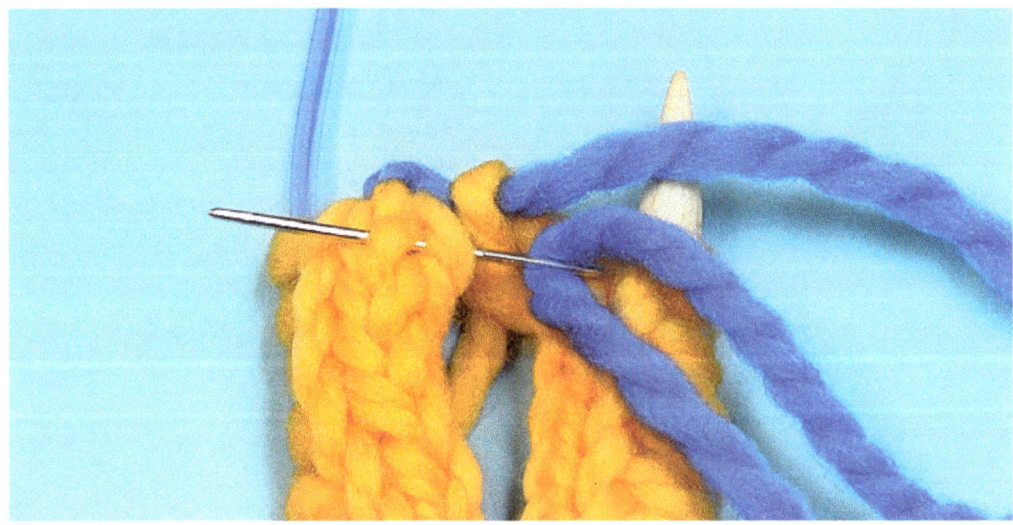

Pull the yarn through, **shaping the next strand** of the seam.

STEP 1

With the working **yarn at the back** of the work and out of the way, insert the wool needle **from back to front** into the first stitch from the tip of the right needle.

Slip this stitch off the knitting needle and pull the yarn through, but **don't pull it too much**. The strand between the two sides of the braid should be **as long as one leg of an average stitch** that forms the braid.

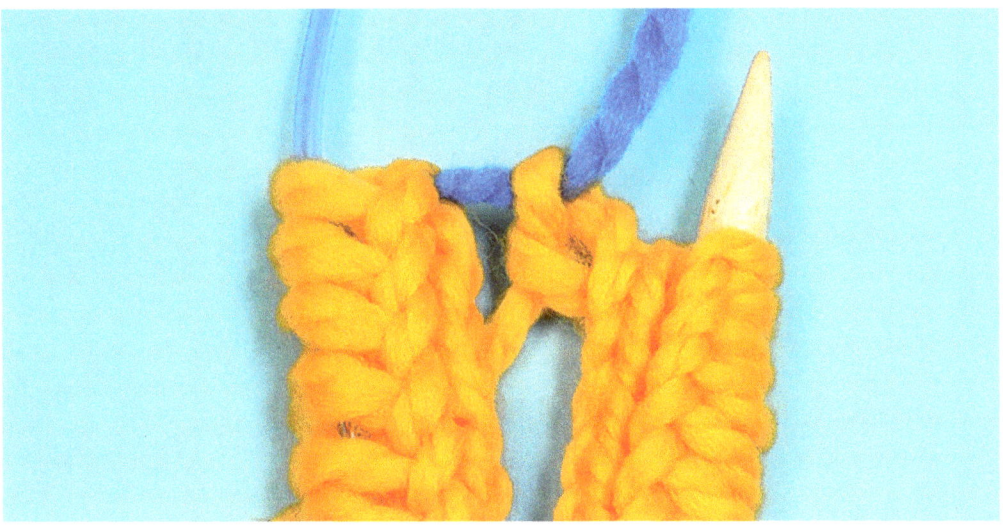

STEP 2

Insert the wool needle **from right to left** under both legs of the first stitch at the right side of the first row of the braid. Because the **braid is now upside down**, this stitch looks like an **inverted "V"**.

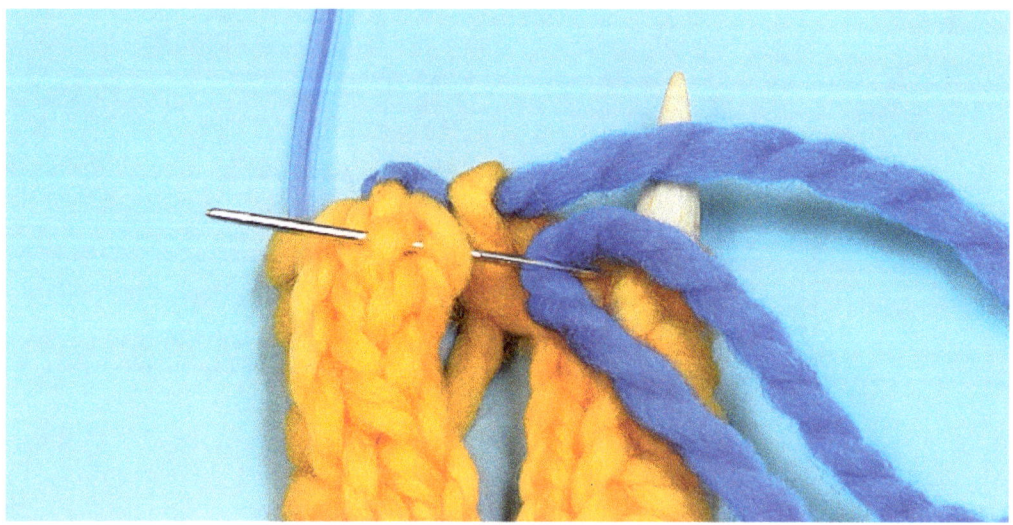

Pull the yarn through, **shaping the next strand** of the seam.

STEP 3

Insert the wool needle **from front to back** into the stitch that we slipped in step 1 and **from back to front** into the next live stitch.

Slip this stitch **off the knitting needle**, pull the yarn through, and **adjust the length of the strand** to make it as long as one leg of an average stitch of the braid.

STEP 4

Now insert the wool needle **from right to left** under both legs of the **second stitch** at the beginning of the braid (another inverted "V").

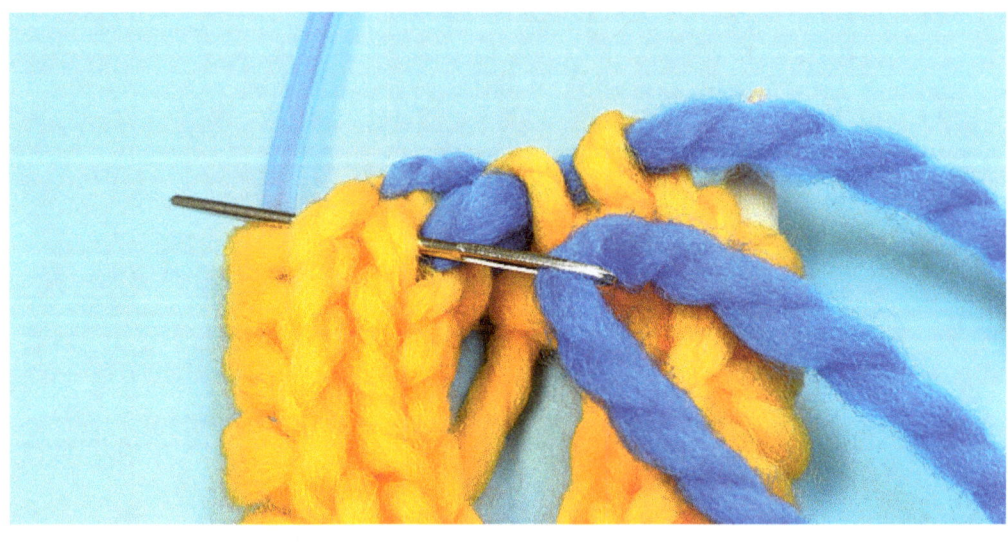

Pull the yarn through and **shape this new strand** of the seam.

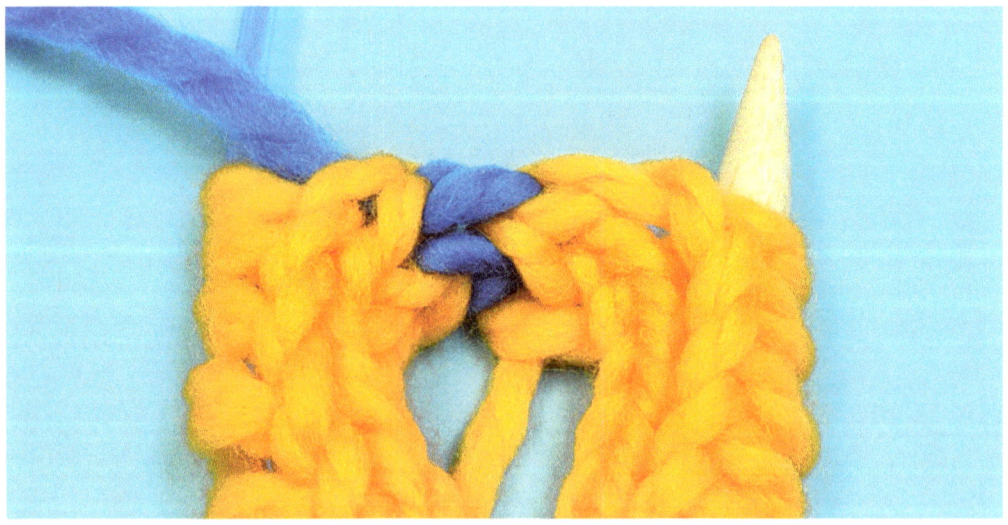

STEP 5

This is the **last step** that we have to perform to give our braid a perfectly seamless look.

Insert the wool needle **from front to back** into the second live stitch of the braid and **from back to front** into the first live stitch of the braid (the stitch that we slipped in step 1).

Pull the yarn through and **shape the last strand** of the seam.

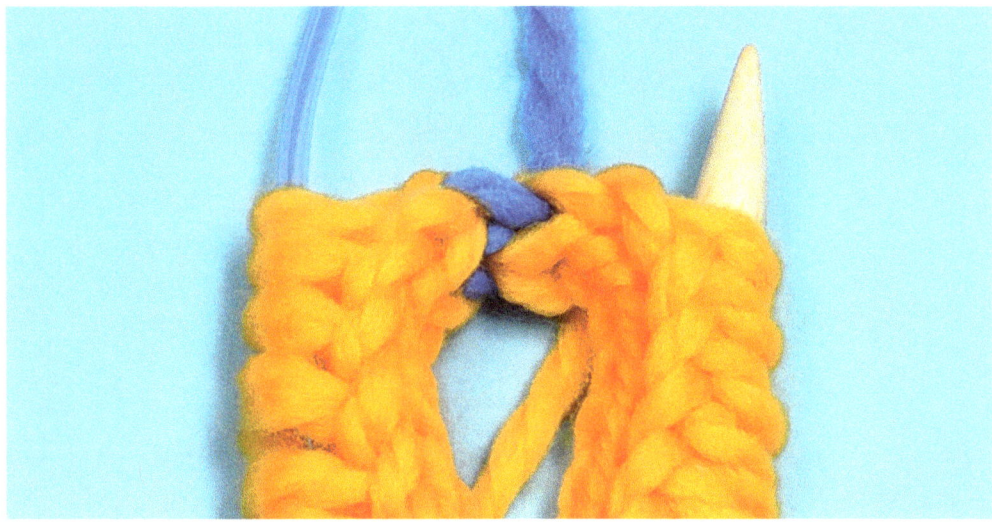

Secure the yarn and **hide the yarn tail** inside the braid.

Now is a good time to **place a marker** while we still remember where the seam is.

When the seam is worked with the **yarn tail in the same colour as the project**, it becomes **absolutely invisible**. The marker will help you recognize where the round begins.

Now, let's see how we can make a **matching braided edge** when we bind off the stitches.

BRAIDED BIND OFF WORKED FLAT

At the beginning of the bind-off row, **cast on two stitches using the knitted cast on** (see page 80 for more details)

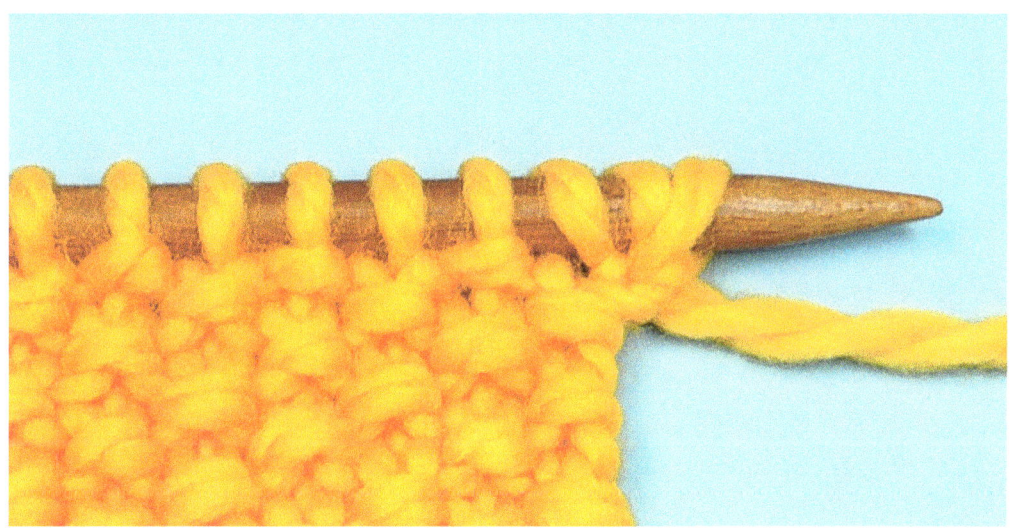

STEP 1

Knit one stitch (it will be the last stitch that you cast on in the previous step).

STEP 2

With the **yarn at the back** of the work, insert the tip of the right needle **from right to left** into the next two stitches (one stitch of the braid and one stitch of the project), and knit these two stitches **together through the back loop**.

STEP 3

With the **yarn still at the back** of the work, slip both stitches of the braid **back to the left needle**. To avoid twisting the stitches, insert the tip of the left needle **from left to right** into each stitch, then take the tip of the right needle out, leaving the stitch on the left needle.

These are the steps that we are going to **repeat**—knit one stitch, knit two stitches together through the back loop, and then slip both stitches back to the left needle.

Work until you have **only two stitches left**. Slip these stitches **to the left needle**, just as we did in step 3.

Cut the yarn, leaving a tail that is about 15cm / 6" long. Thread the **tail into a wool needle**. Run the wool needle **through the last two stitches**.

Slip the stitches off the knitting needle, pull the yarn to **tighten the last stitches**, secure the yarn, and **hide the tail** inside the braid.

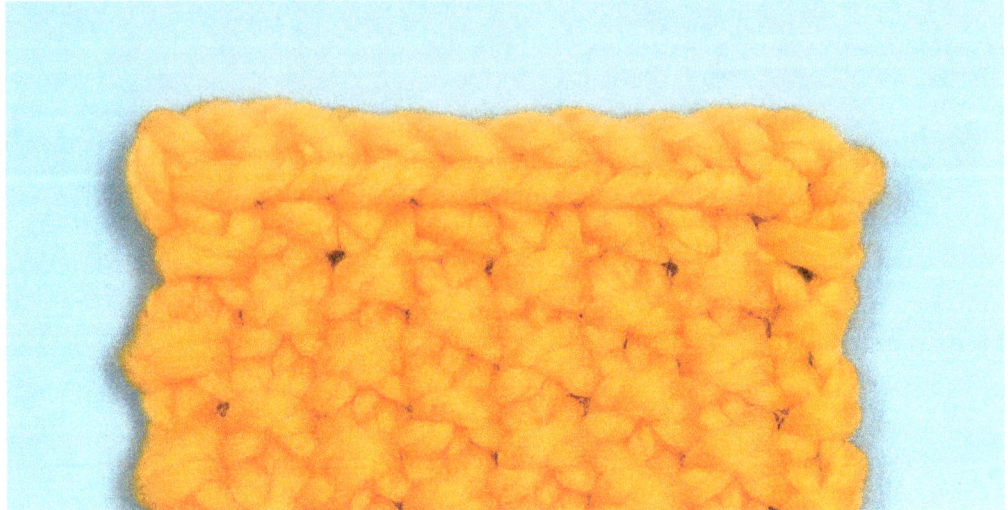

BRAIDED BIND OFF WORKED IN THE ROUND

To bind off stitches of a seamless project, **cast on two stitches** using the knitted cast on method (page 80).

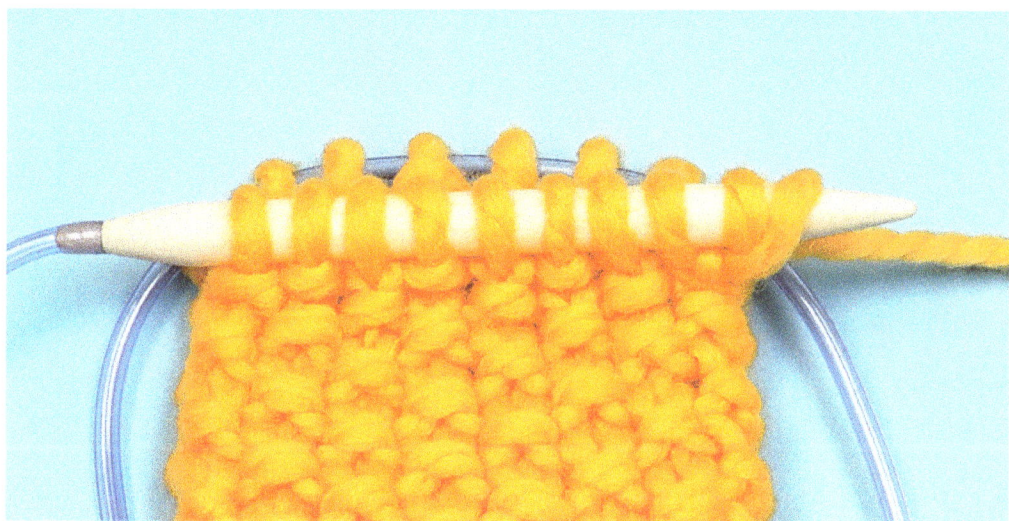

Then repeat the **same three steps** that we followed when we added this edging to a project **worked flat**—knit one stitch, knit the next two stitches together through the back loop, and slip both stitches back to the left needle.

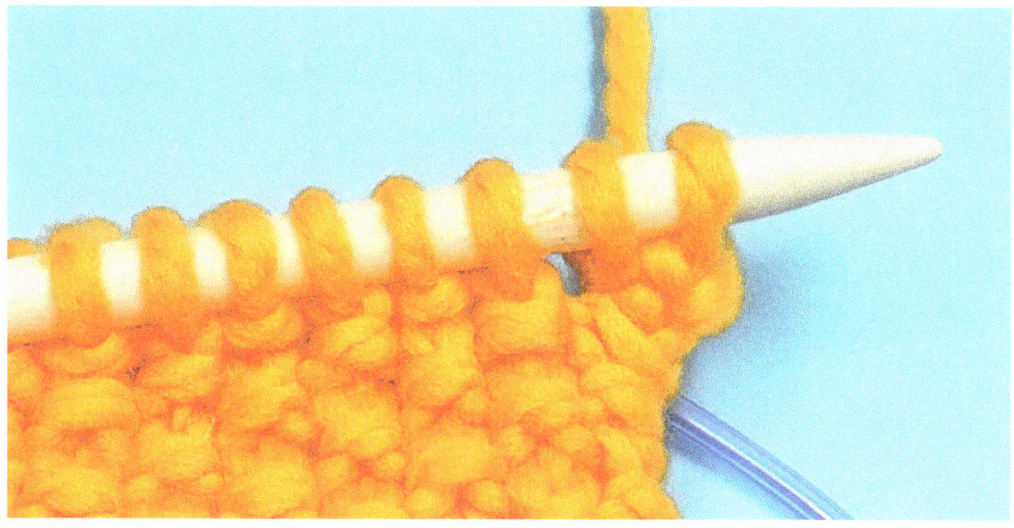

Stop when you have only **two stitches left**. Keep these stitches **on the right needle**.

To make the edge as seamless as the project itself, we should **graft the last two stitches** of the bind off edge **to the first two stitches** of the bind off edge, and now is the time to do this.

Cut the yarn, leaving a tail around 30 cm / 12" long, and **thread this yarn tail into a wool needle**. To make it easier for you to see how the grafting works, I'll use a yarn tail in a contrasting colour.

STEP 1

Insert the wool needle **from back to front** into the first stitch from the tip of the right needle.

Slip the stitch **off the knitting needle** and pull the yarn through. If this stitch is too loose, pull the yarn a bit more to **adjust the size of the stitch**.

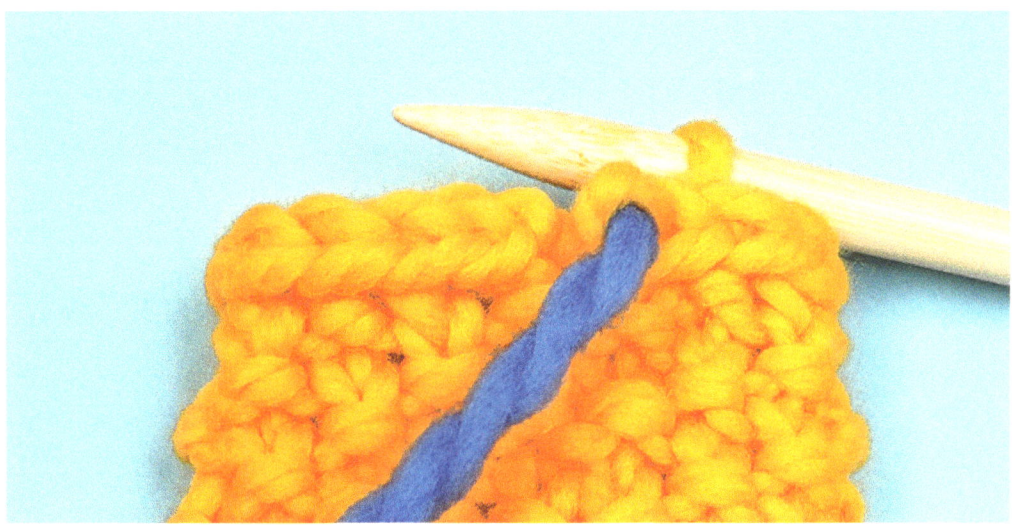

STEP 2

Insert the wool needle **from the bottom up** under both legs of the **corresponding stitch** at the beginning of the bind off edge.

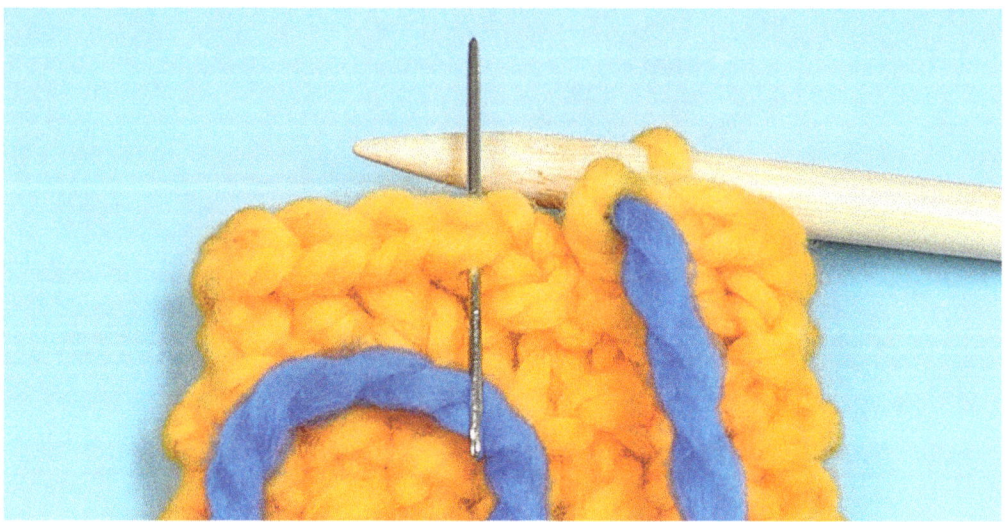

Pull the yarn through, but **don't pull it too tight**—the strand between the two sides of the edge should be as long as one leg of any other stitch that forms the braid.

STEP 3

Insert the wool needle **from front to back** into the stitch that we slipped off the needle in step 1, and **from back to front** into the last stitch on the knitting needle.

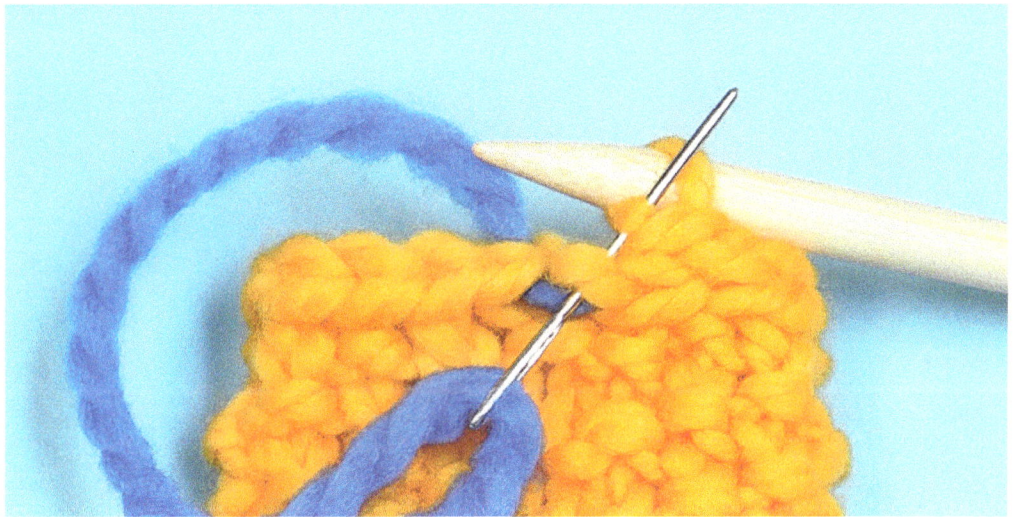

Slip the stitch off the knitting needle, pull the yarn through, and **shape another strand** of the invisible seam.

STEP 4

Insert the wool needle **under both legs of the second stitch** at the beginning of the bind off edge.

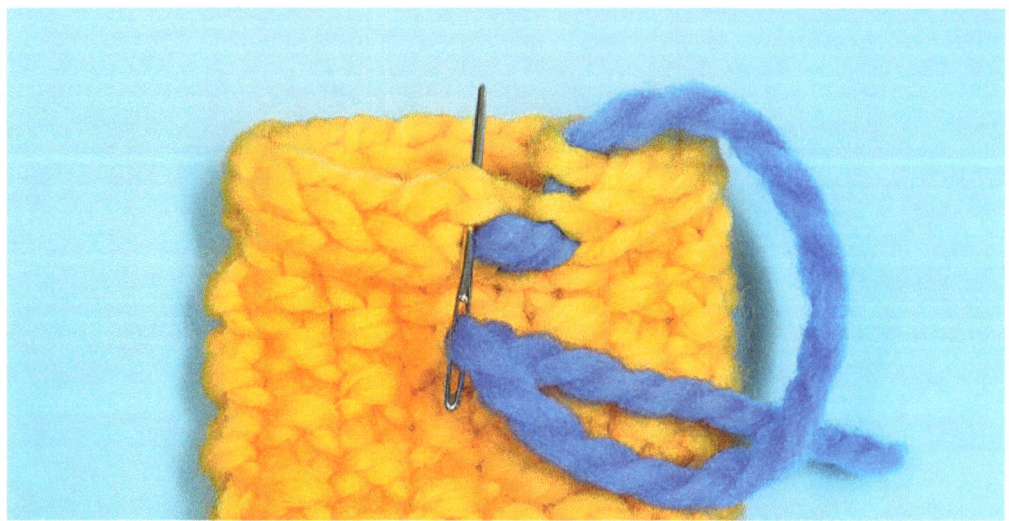

Pull the yarn through and **adjust the length of the strand**.

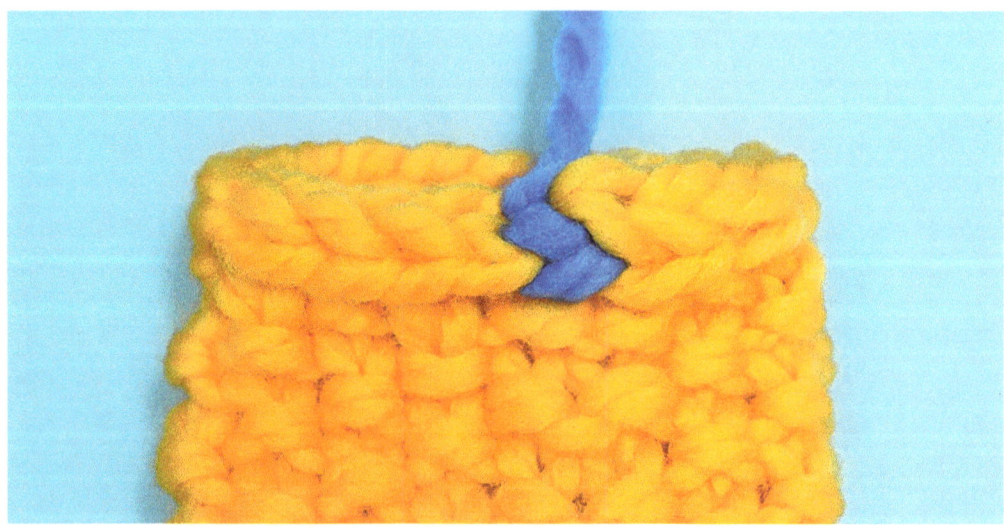

STEP 5

Finally, insert the wool needle **from the top down** into the second live stitch (the stitch that we slipped off the needle in step 3).

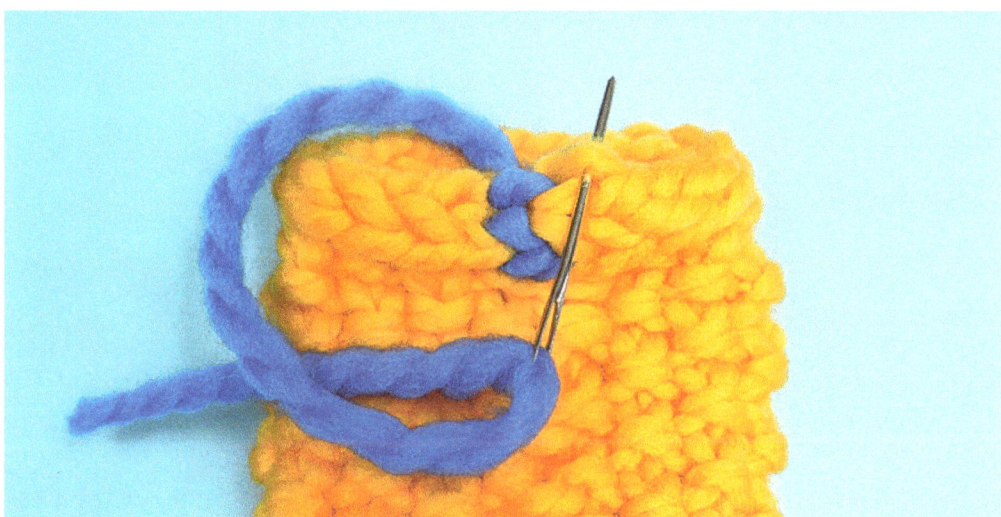

Pull the yarn through, forming a stitch that looks **similar to the rest of the stitches** of the bind off edge. Secure the yarn and **hide the tail** inside the braid.

When the grafting is made with **yarn in the same colour** as the project, the seam is **completely invisible**.

As you see, the edge doesn't have a right or a wrong side. It is **identical on both sides** of the fabric.

The beautiful braid that decorates three sides of the edge will look great on **necklines, sleeves, and bottom edges** of a top-down sweater, or any other project that you decide to treat with a braided bind off.

Quick reference card

I-CORD CAST ON

Use any cast on method you like to cast on 3 to 5 stitches for the future i-cord.

Move the yarn from the back to the front of the right needle to make a reverse yarn over.

Knit the stitches of the i-cord.

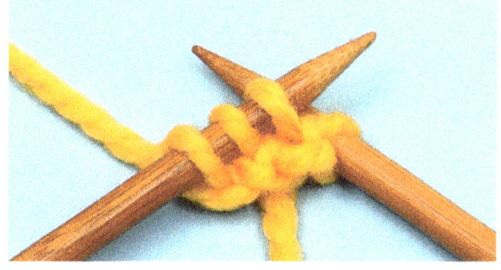

Slip the stitches of the i-cord purlwise to the left needle.

Repeat until you cast on the number of stitches that you need minus 1 stitch (excluding the stitches of the I-cord).

Knit the stitches of the I-cord together. In the first row, knit or purl stitches as usual, through the front loop.

Quick reference card

I-CORD BIND OFF

At the beginning of a right-side row, cast on 3 to 5 stitches for the i-cord using knitted cast on.

Knit stitches one by one until you get to the last stitch of the i-cord.

Knit the last stitch of the i-cord together with one stitch of the main fabric through the back loop.

Slip the resulting stitches purlwise to the left needle.

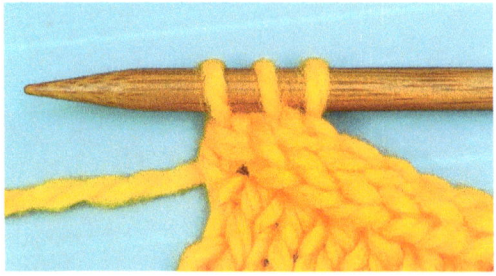

Repeat until you bind off all stitches of the main fabric and there are only the stitches of the i-cord left on the right needle.

Cut the yarn, thread the yarn tail into a wool needle, and run it through the last stitches. Pull tight and secure the yarn.

Quick reference card

PURLED I-CORD CAST ON

Use any cast on method you like to cast on 3 to 5 stitches for the future i-cord.

Move the yarn from the front to the back of the right needle to make a yarn over.

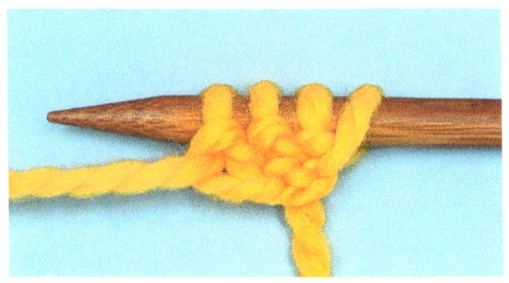

Purl the stitches of the i-cord.

Slip the stitches of the i-cord purlwise to the left needle.

Repeat until you cast on the number of stitches that you need minus 1 stitch (excluding the stitches of the i-cord).

Turn the work and purl the stitches of the I-cord together.. In the first row, knit or purl stitches through the back loop.

I-CORD EDGES | 161

Quick reference card

PURLED I-CORD BIND OFF

At the beginning of a right-side row, cast on 3 to 5 stitches for the i-cord using knitted cast on.

Purl stitches one by one until you get to the last stitch of the i-cord.

Purl the last stitch of the i-cord together with one stitch of the main fabric.

Bring the yarn to the back and slip the resulting stitches purlwise to the left needle.

Repeat until you bind off all stitches of the main fabric and there are only the stitches of the i-cord left on the right needle.

Cut the yarn, thread the yarn tail into a wool needle, and run it through the last stitches. Pull tight and secure the yarn.

Quick reference card

BRAIDED CAST ON

Use any cast on method you like to cast on 2 stitches for the future braid.

Move the yarn from the back to the front of the right needle to make a reverse yarn over.

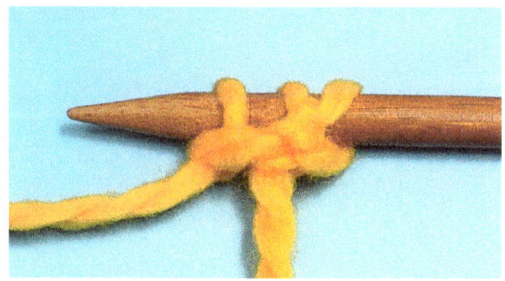

Knit 2 stitches.

Slip 2 stitches purlwise to the left needle.

Repeat until you cast on the number of stitches that you need minus 1 stitch (excluding the stitches of the braid).

Pass the second stitch on the left needle over the first one, then slip the remaining stitch to the right needle.

Quick reference card

BRAIDED BIND OFF

Use the knitted cast on method to cast on 2 stitches for the future braid.

Knit 1 stitch.

Knit the last stitch of the braid together with one stitch of the main fabric through the back loop.

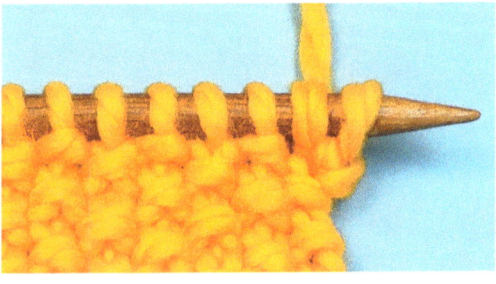

Slip both stitches purlwise to the left needle.

Repeat until you bind off all stitches of the main fabric and there are only 2 stitches on your left needle.

Cut the yarn, thread the yarn tail into a wool needle, and run it through the last stitches. Pull tight and secure the yarn.

THIS CONCLUDES THE FIRST PART OF THE BOOK

In the second part, we'll talk about pairs of matching cast on and bind off methods that turn the edges of our projects into decorative elements. These are the edges that transform even a most basic of projects into an exquisite creation.

We'll see how we can make the picot edging that designers add to their most well-crafted knits. Then we'll take the idea of decorative edgings one step further when we discuss edges formed by criss-cross and scalloped cast on and bind off methods.

Finally, we'll talk about the edges that do not look like edges. They do not end at the top or at the bottom of a project. Rather, they seem to be flowing around the fabric continuously.

The second part of the book is set to be published in November 2024.

Stay tuned!

Maryna

There are more
knitting methods
to explore at
www.10rowsaday.com

www.ingramcontent.com/pod-product-compliance
Lightning Source LLC
Chambersburg PA
CBHW042035100526
44587CB00030B/4431